I Am My Own Wife

I Am My Own Wife

The True Story of Charlotte von Mahlsdorf

CHARLOTTE VON MAHLSDORF

Translated by Jean Hollander

With photographs by Burkhard Peter

CLEIS
PRESS

Published in the United States by Cleis Press Inc.,
P.O. Box 14684, San Francisco, California 94114.

Cover design: Scott Idleman / Blink
Book design: Karen Quigg
Cover Photo: Burkhard Peter
Cleis Press logo art: Juana Alicia

Printed in the United States.

TRANSLATOR'S NOTE

I would like to thank Regine Weisert for her helpful solutions to some knotty problems,
and Robert Hollander for his careful reading of my text. This translation is dedicated to
N., who died while I was at work on this text, and whom I loved.

Library of Congress Cataloging-in-Publication Data

Mahlsdorf, Charlotte von, 1928–2000
   [Ich bin meine eigene Frau. English]
   I am my own wife : the true story of Charlotte von Mahlsdorf / Charlotte von
Mahlsdorf ; with photographs by Burkhard Peter ; translated by Jean Hollander.
     p. cm.
   ISBN 1-57344-200-3 (pbk.)
   1. Mahlsdorf, Charlotte von, 1928– 2. Transvestites—Germany—Berlin—
Biography. 3. Gay men—Germany—Berlin—Biography. 4. Mahlsdorf (Berlin,
Germany)—Biography. 5. National socialism—Germany—Berlin. 6. Gründerzeit
Museum (Mahlsdorf, Berlin, Germany) 7. Furniture—Germany—Berlin—Collectors
and collecting. 8. Art objects—Germany—Berlin—Collectors and collecting.
9. Architecture—Conservation and restoration—Germany—Berlin. I. Peter,
Burkhard, 1961– II. Hollander, Jean, 1928– III. Title.
   HQ77.8.M34A313 2004
   306.77'8'092—dc22   2004009769

Chapter 1

THIRTY SKINHEADS were descending on Mahlsdorf brandishing iron bars, starter pistols, and torn-out fence slats.

I had been looking at the garden from one of the windows of the Gründerzeit Museum. The paper moons we had hung from the clotheslines were tossing in the wind. The eighty or so guests still there were lightheartedly celebrating the coming of spring. The Tina Turner lookalike had already removed her make-up. The belly dancer no longer gyrated for the guests, but was mingling with them at the cocktail bar. Sausages sizzled on the grill. Gays and lesbians were dancing, and the moon shone through the trees of the park like a scene from a kitchy picture postcard.

It was May Day 1991. My co-worker Beate and I had been kept busy the whole evening showing guests from near and far through the museum every half hour. I decided to put out the lights and have a quick look outside.

I had barely extinguished the last lamp when I heard the sharp sound of splintering glass, a noise I have been allergic to for over fifty-four years. A young man, pale as a corpse, burst into the museum, "Call the cops!"

The Neo-Nazis were flailing away at the guests. Everything was happening with terrific speed. From close range with a flare gun, one particularly brave guy shot my second co-worker Sylvia in the face, right near the eye. A young woman from Munich wasn't so lucky: he managed to hit her eye, badly damaging the retina. Then someone smashed a fence slat over the head of an eighteen-year-old girl.

Screams and groans mixed with the crash of the bandstand being attacked by the rabble and the wrecking of the info-stalls the gay group from East Berlin had erected.

Now the bomber-jackets were storming the dance floor. There, like a lighthouse, stood a transvestite, wearing a fancy dress and a huge red hat. They were going to beat him up, but hesitated, like the cowards they were, because he too had armed himself with a fence slat. Enveloped by a stream of floodlights, he called out to the rabble, "Why

I

are you such animals?" He said it twice, and suddenly, they stopped and looked at each other in bewilderment. Somebody yelled, "Here come the cops!" and the young Nazis took off like a stampeding herd of cattle, emptying their ammunition into the neighboring recycling dump. A thousand tons of old paper went up in flames. Everybody was screaming and getting in each other's way. The fire brigade drove up with fifty men, put the fire out and took the wounded to the hospital—it was chaos.

I had run out, hatchet in hand. Sylvia and Beate stopped me and told me it was all over. They grabbed me and dragged me back inside. They knew that if I had gotten my hands on someone, I would have hauled off without considering the consequences.

An hour later, I went into the garden with a flashlight. I looked at the wrecked stands, the shattered bottles, the demolished phonograph, and the smashed juke box. As I swept broken glass from the cellar door panes off the road, I was reminded of another scene so very much like this one.

I was on the streetcar going through Mahlsdorf-Süd in the direction of Köpenick. Looking out the window, I saw that Egona's grocery store and the soap shop owned by Wasservogel, the Jew, had both been wrecked. Cohn's shop in Köpenick no longer had window panes. The streetcar stopped in the old part of town, right across from a fabric shop. The young owner, tears streaming down her face, was gathering together the remnants of her goods. Three SA men, legs spread apart, were standing by, "You Jewish sow, now you're finally gonna learn to work!" I was so angry, I clenched my hands around the safety pole. The men kicked the woman's hip with their heavy boots. She fell on the broken glass. The trolley went on. By the time I got home from school, all the stores were boarded up. It was the morning of the tenth of November, 1938.

At home, the maid was describing how the Nazis wreaked havoc in other stores owned by Jews. "Mr. Brauner," she said to my great-uncle in a voice shaking with anger, "you have no idea how Tietz's and Wertheim's and Brandmann's shops were wrecked. At Brandmann's, they threw all the big clocks through the display windows out into the street. And the SA men went at the glass cases with their boots and threw the weights—those heavy weights—on top of the dials, and filled their pockets with gold and jewels! What a disgrace!"

Could that be true? The firm of Brandmann, famous throughout Berlin, destroyed? I had always listened to their advertisements on the radio with such pleasure. First you heard *ding! dong!* followed by the ad for Brandmann clocks in Münzstrasse. My uncle and I had often gone past their shop. How I loved seeing those beautiful clocks in the window!

Instinctively, my uncle began to whisper, "Emmi, keep all that to yourself, we have to be careful. Who knows what's still to come." Yes, my great-uncle was wise to say that. I owe him a great deal. Ten years before, in Mahlsdorf, a dreamy village at the eastern edge of Berlin, on Sunday, March 18, 1928, I first saw the light of day. I, Lothar Berfelde.

Chapter 2

THE BERFELDE FAMILY is descended from an old Markish aristocratic line first mentioned in a 1285 chronicle as the founders of the village of Berfelde, today called Beerfelde, near Fürstenwalde. With the passing centuries, the spelling of our name changed from Berfelde to Beerfeld, Baerfelde, Berfeldt, and finally, Beerfeldt. The family crest, however, remained unchanged: a shield divided in the center, with one star against a blue background, the other against a silver one.

My genealogy resulted from a misalliance in the middle of the eighteenth century. One of my ancestors, an officer in the Prussian army, had married the daughter of a fisherman, something simply not done at the time. As "dimmed" nobility, we kept our crest, but lost our "von."

The descendants of the aristocratic branch of the von Beerfelde line, to whom I'm only distantly related, were in possession of the castle and manor house Zuchen near Zanow, in the area of Köslin in Pomerania, until 1907.

Bertha von Beerfelde, the head of this family and mother of nine children, had a hard time of it. Her husband, Rittmeister Rudolf von Beerfelde, a Schwedter dragoon, was thrown and crushed by his horse during maneuvers. After a fire in 1905, followed by loss of livestock and bad crops the next year, Bertha von Beerfelde decided to sell her holdings and to divide the proceeds among her nine children. The buyer, a mill-owner from Zanow, brought the money in cash—two and a half million goldmarks! Mother and children, buyer, and the messengers with the money were all seated in the ballroom of the palace. The forester had also been invited. He stood with loaded gun at the ready in case something should go wrong.

Two-hundred and fifty thousand goldmarks each, dealt out by the accountants, were placed on the table in front of every one of the nine children, as well as the mother. Then she stood up and said, "Be frugal and increase your share."

One of her sons, a captain in the Alexander regiment and a Prussian Officer, Hans-Georg von Beerfelde, filled with burning patriotism and

5

love for the Kaiser, had enlisted in the First World War. Courageous and fanatically devoted to truth, he saw the light after a few years when that hopeless war, getting more and more hopeless each day, was taken over by Hindenburg, the "hero of Tannenberg," and the power-serving First Quartermaster General Ludendorff.

Beerfelde went to see the Kaiser, "It is not a good idea to send students with only three weeks of training to fight at the front where even an experienced soldier has a difficult time." The Kaiser examined my uncle coldly with narrowed eyes and pursed lips. He stared grimly at this man who had dared to criticize him at a general staff meeting called to discuss the war.

After the battle of Langemarck, at which a good part of the flower of German youth was mowed down—according to witnesses the horrible screams of the young for their fathers and mothers resounded from the battlefield—Captain Beerfelde had himself announced to his commander-in-chief. On that day, Colonel Graf von Plüskow was on duty in the ante-chamber. He greeted Beerfelde anxiously with the words, "His Majesty is not in a good mood. I hope you do not have anything unpleasant to report."

"Only the truth," my uncle answered meaningfully. He was permitted to enter. His majesty was seated at a desk embellished with bronze fittings. He spread his hands and asked, "Well, my dear Beerfelde, what have you come to tell me?"

My uncle was not inclined to honor the motto "Majesty requires sunshine" in his dealings with the Kaiser. "Your Majesty, this is no longer a war, this is murder!"

The Kaiser became as red as a beet. Nobody had ever dared to speak that way to his face. "Beerfelde, how dare you, a Prussian Officer, utter such words!" But my uncle did not allow himself to be intimidated. The exchange between Kaiser and captain became so sharp and the shouting so furious that Plüskow, standing outside the door, grew pale.

My uncle ripped his officer's epaulettes from his uniform and threw them at the feet of Wilhelm II. "This is my last day as an officer!"

"That is desertion," snorted the Kaiser. My uncle simply left him standing there, and rushed out, slamming the door with a loud crash.

Plüskow, who was always well disposed towards my uncle, looked at him with a mingling of shock and pity. "I have to order you taken into custody. Desertion means a war tribunal and the death sentence."

"I really felt sorry for the old gentleman at that moment," my uncle said, telling me the story later, as if he still had no idea in what danger he had been.

A few weeks after the duel of words between the Kaiser and the Captain, Plüskow appeared in the military prison at Lehrter Strasse in Berlin and informed my uncle that the Kaiser was prepared to forget everything, if he, Beerfelde, would formally apologize. Wilhelm II did not want to overdramatize the event and lose one of his best officers. "If anybody has to apologize, it is the emperor, not I," was the answer. "What I said is the truth and I stand by it. And I'm willing to die for it."

Beerfelde used his time in prison to compose a pamphlet entitled *Michel, Wake Up!* which caused a scandal. Based on information supplied by Count Lichnowsky, the former German ambassador to London, he disclosed the false documentation of the German *White Book* of 1914 which represented the causes of the First World War in much too favorable a light for Germany: it alleged that Germany, surrounded by enemies, had been forced into war.

Only the November revolution of 1918 prevented my uncle from being brought before the military tribunal. Some workers stormed the military prison and carried Beerfelde on their shoulders past the gate. He became a member of the revolutionary committee and gave inspiring speeches in Zirkus Busch where Friedrich Ebert, more reluctant than enthusiastic, was chosen president of the people's party by workers and soldiers.

Tall, with penetrating eyes under bushy brows, my uncle possessed the aura of a guru. As with all torchbearers, there was something fanatic about him. He went so far as to have Minister of War Scheuch arrested without consulting anyone. Beerfelde held to the view that a minister of war was unnecessary once the war was over. Because of this arbitrary decision, he was expelled from the revolutionary committee. A German revolution had to run along orderly tracks.

My uncle withdrew to his apartment where he designed and printed postcards on which the poem "Our Father of the Revolution" appeared. He sent the first card to the Kaiser, who had abdicated and was staying at Schloss Amerongen in Holland. He naturally did not receive an answer.

Editor, typesetter, and printer all in one, he produced his own revolutionary newspaper, *The Red Torch*. He delivered the papers to newspaper vendors on his bicycle. He allowed them to pocket the sales price of five pennies. The gist of his message was that Christ was the first communist. My uncle was of the opinion that socialism should be reconciled with Christianity. Thus, he fell between two stools. Although a believer, he forfeited the support of the Church, who were suspicious of "red" tendencies; and he lost out with the socialists who thought him too pious.

Among the nobility he was known as "the red Beerfelde" or "the red Captain." He had like-minded friends in Helmut von Gerlach and the writer Ludwig Renn, whose real name was Baron Arnold Vieth von Golssenau and who had harshly rejected his blue-blood rank with his book *Nobility in Decline*.

When the Nazis usurped power and it became clear that Germany would again be militarized, my uncle, more and more the naïve savior of the world, wrote to the Führer, "If you again institute the draft after this horrible war, you will be committing a crime against the German people." The answer from Berlin was prompt. If he didn't stop his "imbecilic writing," the Nazis threatened, in legal terminology that was nonetheless quite clear, he would be liquidated.

One morning in 1935, the Gestapo forced their way into his house in Lindau at the Bodensee and carried him off to Munich for interrogation. SS men beat and cudgeled him until he lost consciousness. He awoke in a barrack in KZ Dachau. He can presumably thank his international reputation and the fact that the Nazis thought him a harmless madman for his release four years later.

After the war, having become a radical pacifist, he founded the Bureau of Peace, Friendship and Understanding Among Nations and wrote letters to Roosevelt, Truman, Churchill, De Gaulle, and Stalin.

When I got to know Uncle Hans-Georg after the war, I sensed an immediate affinity between us. Hearing the story of his life, I was impressed with his courage and love of truth. I have inherited none, or very little of his terrible temper—he once threatened me with a cane for being five minutes late. I take after his brother Curt, who with delicate feminine features was the very image of his mother. He was an officer and a bachelor.

Chapter 3

MY MOTHER WAS THE GOOD FAIRY in my life. She was a warm-hearted woman with firm principles. If anyone flouted them, she would get angry and strike the table with the flat of her hand. During the Nazi rule, she never voted in elections because the results were predetermined. That kind of behavior was not without its dangers, but she didn't care.

Our intellectual and spiritual relationship was very close from the day she read me my first bedtime story until her death in 1991. My mother had what many people today lack: innate tact. I absorbed this trait from her. When I reflect upon it, I realize that I am the very image of my mother. "You know, Mutti," I declared when I was twenty, "I am really your oldest daughter." She laughed, "Oh, don't talk such nonsense!"

Later I read her passages from a book by Dr. Magnus Hirschfeld, the famous scholar who, in the twenties, had founded the first institute for research into sexual behavior. When it became clear to her that I felt myself to be a woman to my very soul, she said, "You know, as a real woman, it is hard for me to empathize with you about that. But if it makes you happy, that's the main thing."

Even as a young boy I admired her beautiful garments. Often when she went out she wore an ultramarine evening dress and I imagined how beautiful she would look, standing under a splendid chandelier at a soirée. She did not wear make-up; at most she powdered her nose a little. Everything about her was modest and unassuming, like the simple necklace she wore for special occasions.

Named Gretchen Gaupp, she was born into a merchant family in Markgröningen near Ludwigsburg. Her father died when she was eight weeks old. Her mother then went to live with her brother at Cannstatt near Stuttgart. He was an auto engineer working for Gottlieb Daimler. In 1899, under the technical direction of Wilhelm Maybach, my great-uncle designed and constructed a motor, a frame and a body which, when mounted together, became the Mercedes, making the name of Consul Jellinek's daughter famous even today.

My mother was driven to her christening in 1902 in a Daimler, creating quite a stir in a small town such as Markgröningen. Many townspeople, when they saw that motorized monster roaring down the main street, fled into the side streets shouting, "The devil is coming! The devil is coming in his carriage!"

Later my mother studied at the lyceum. She enjoyed, as we so nicely put it, the education of a daughter of the upper classes. In 1923, she came to Mahlsdorf to live with my grandmother, my great-uncle, and his sister.

She took to the notion of standing on her own two feet, something of a novelty then for a socially secure woman—my great-uncle was definitely well-to-do. At that time, only poor girls went to work. My mother wanted to learn stenography and begin a career as secretary to a lawyer. When she introduced herself at the lawyer's office, he asked her, "Miss Gaupp, why do you want to take a position from a girl without means? You don't need to work." After she had thought about it, my mother agreed with him. "Yes, why shouldn't a girl who needs the pay more than I work here?" Today that seems unbelievable, but that's how things were.

My great-uncle came from Lettowitz, near Brünn. In the mid-nineteenth century the family had been in the lace and curtain business, and his father, an expert weaver, had continued to specialize in the manufacture of lace fabrics using wooden machines, since industrialization was slow catching on in Germany. Eventually his business did so well that he was able to go to England to buy machines made of steel, which he transported across the Channel on a sidewheel steamer. But in 1866, it all came to a sudden end. Fire destroyed his factory and insurance against this kind of mishap was unknown at the time. The family left and took up residence in Vienna. After the death of his father, my great-uncle took care of his three sisters. Later, he moved to Germany and began to work for Daimler in 1898. He settled in Berlin in 1908 and started to develop motor-cars for the firm of Bergmann.

Of conservative appearance—although he could not hide his Bohemian heritage—he wanted nothing to do with nationalism, particularly in its perverted Nazi version. In addition to having had an education in the humanities (he knew Greek, Latin, and French) he was also an excellent mathematician. And even though he designed radically new automobiles and believed in progress, he always remained a man of the nineteenth century in thought, feeling, and attitude. I can still see him clearly in his pinstripe suit (old-fashioned even then), vest, golden pocketwatch on a chain, tie pin in his cravat, cuffs and collar-studs, bristly haircut and pince-nez, through which he would pensively regard me with kind, blue-gray eyes.

At that time, a woman had to be married by twenty-five because at thirty, she was considered an old hag. My uncle decided to advertise for a prospective bridegroom for my mother in 1927.

A perfectly guileless being, he was absurdly unequipped to choose the right man for my mother. He could readily judge whether a young engineer was qualified to work in his office, but he knew too little of evil to evaluate the character of a potential husband. He saw only the good in a person—a weakness to which now and then I also succumb. "But circumstances just ain't so," as Brecht has Peachum sing in the *Threepenny Opera.*

Several suitors answered the advertisement and my uncle made his choice, of course a bad one.

After their wedding, my parents moved into the upper floor of the cottage. It was a very unhappy marriage because my father was a brutal tyrant with a riding-crop mentality. After only half a year, my mother wanted a divorce. My father almost killed her when he found out.

It was horrible. My mother didn't dare tell my father to his face of her intention to divorce him. She was afraid—with good reason—of further mistreatment. So my uncle wrote my father a letter, dated November 2, 1927, in which he politely but firmly informed him that my mother wished to divorce him and that he should vacate the house.

My father read the letter that evening when he returned from work. My mother had wisely withdrawn to my great-uncle's rooms. My father came storming down the stairs, made a scene, threw the letter at my great-uncle's feet and raced upstairs, slamming the door so hard that the stained-glass window broke. A few minutes later he burst in again, this time with his revolver. It's hard to believe, but he actually took a shot at my mother, and if my uncle had not been there and pushed his arm up, I would not be here today. The bullet is still lodged in the ceiling of the house where I was born.

Chapter 4

EVEN AS A SMALL CHILD I thought my father a fiend, although I was too young to know how brutally he was abusing my mother. But small children understand things. I recall him giving me a horrible beating over some trifle, screeching barrack obscenities all the while. When I cried, he roared, "Boys don't cry!" and hit me harder. That was my father, Max Berfelde.

The son of a fisherman, a descendant of the Lossower line of the family, he was born in 1888 in Frankfurt an der Oder about a hundred years after that untoward union with the fisherman's daughter. In the First World War, he copied the aristocratic branch of our family—the Sommerfelds, to whom my distant relative Hans-Georg von Beerfelde belonged—and became a soldier. After the end of the war, he was employed by an important nitrogen syndicate.

An event occurred in 1930 that reveals my father's violent temperament. He had a falling-out with a colleague, an extremely amiable man according to my mother. Father grabbed him by the shoulders and shoved him so hard through one of the tall windows of the building that broken glass and part of the window frame crashed to the sidewalk. The putty holding the upper pane gave way and the glass slid down, pinning in the unfortunate man. The firm was located on the fourth floor, and the man was left with three quarters of his body dangling outside the window. Firemen arrived and spread a net, while others succeeded in freeing him. My father received a reprimand and was assigned to another department.

He seemed a man without history. There were not even traces of close relatives, no photos, no letters, no pictures: a man without a past, or one who had thrust aside his past because it gnawed at his soul. One time however, in a burst of confidence, while we stood on the Milchrampe in Motzen, he told me about his parents. His mother had been a devil in human form. Once, she ran after an apprentice for a supposed misdeed like a goddess of vengeance, brandishing an axe high in her hands. Terror-stricken, the fourteen-year-old rascal jumped into the Oder. Since she could not swim, she stopped at the furthest plank, furiously stamping on the wood; beside herself with rage, she threw the axe after the lad. She barely missed. Her husband, the fisherman Wilhelm Berfelde, was a quiet, thoughtful man. If things were stormy at home, he took off in his boat and found peace in nature.

Although my father enlisted as an ordinary soldier in the First World War, his ambition and pride permitted him to dream of a military career as a non-commissioned officer. But when the war ended, he was still an ordinary soldier, and I assume this is when things fell apart for him. Since he couldn't give orders on the parade ground, he gave orders at home. We were the recruits he could oppress to his heart's content. His tone was always militaristic, "Now I order you...," and his close-set eyes—I don't know their color anymore because I never wanted to meet his gaze—blazed with a touch of madness. Even as a small boy, I asked myself in despair how could I possibly ever help my mother. A child doesn't know he will grow strong and one day be capable of action.

The sounds that penetrated from the upper story to the lower floor are indelibly engraved in my mind: my father yapping and bellowing, oak chairs crashing as he shoved my mother around the room, dull thuds when he grabbed and hit her.

When I think about my childhood, I am sometimes surprised that I am not a complete imbecile, so often did my father let me have it with his fists.

By the end of the twenties, he had already joined the National Socialist party and proudly declared himself an "old warrior." After the Nazi take-over, he succeeded in becoming the political leader of Mahlsdorf, until his uncontrollable temper got to be too much even for the Nazis, and they got rid of him.

From early childhood on, I was forced to endure his mad ambition of raising me to be a "young warrior." This extended to absurd corrections of my appearance; for example, if the rain frizzed my hair into small curls, he ordered me to put my head under cold water and comb it down flat. My hair had to be short and neatly parted in military style.

But I was far from being a young warrior. I didn't even feel like a boy. No, I was a girl. I recall a large soirée with ladies and gentlemen of the upper class. The elegant women were magnificently attired, draped with necklaces, chains, and bracelets. I sat on the lap of a distant relative whom I always called Aunt Annie, admiring her dress and jewelry. *I am a little girl*, I told myself, *Someday I will look just like those ladies, and move as gracefully as they.*

I was really only interested in the outfits of my female classmates. If I played with them and their dollhouses, or they with me and my doll furniture, I only thought, *My God, what a pretty bodice this one is wearing!* or *What a lovely flared skirt and what beautifully embroidered trimming!*

I was much more aroused by boys—I liked to look at their bodies and was immediately aware if they looked enticing; with girls, on the other hand, I always paid attention to what kind of shoes or stockings they were wearing, and the styling of their dresses. Over and over I said to myself, *How stupid that I can't wear something like that marvelous bodice, black set off with green, and laced up the front with ribbons through little brass loops.*

At home, when the family albums were brought out with pictures showing my relatives proudly posed against some railing or in front of a flower stand dating from the seventies of the last century, I automatically looked at the draped ladies and, above all, at their smartly tailored dresses. I wanted to wear just such outfits. Eventually I was able to fulfill this desire.

Chapter 5

When I was five or six I preferred to play with old junk rather than real toys. True, I would sometimes pass the time with the doll furniture my mother had given me, or the train set, which had been a present from my great-uncle. But what I really enjoyed was cleaning and admiring my great-uncle's old clocks, kerosene lamps, paintings, and candlesticks.

I spent a great deal of time wandering around Mahlsdorf with a schoolfriend. An extraordinarily rich collection of discarded, out-of-fashion household goods had been dumped where the new school now stands. One day, I came home radiant with joy because I had retrieved an undamaged plate clock. It looked like a painted, blue-white porcelain dish with Roman numerals. A metal box at the back contained the mechanism. Of course, I didn't know anything about clocks then. My watchmaking skills amounted to zero. But as I was tinkering with it, the clock suddenly began to tick again.

My passion for collecting things began on its own, without urging from anyone. My mother tolerated it, surely thinking that if the child enjoyed this hobby, why not? My great-uncle found it good, probably hoping that I would follow in his footsteps as a mechanical engineer one day. But soon he noticed that my interests were mainly focused on household articles. One day, when he saw me begin to dust and polish the furniture as I usually did on coming home from school, he said, "Here you are at your dusting again."

"Yes," I answered, "it has to be done so everything is neat."

My great-uncle looked at me thoughtfully and then his features brightened. "Child, you should have been a girl in 1900. Then I would have hired you as a servant. You would have been a pearl!" A smile spread across his face; I believe that he had, even then, guessed that this boy was really a girl.

My interest in furniture was awakened, even if I still could not tell one period from another. But, for furniture from the post-Biedermeier era, the Gründerzeit, I quickly developed a sixth sense. Columns, lathe-turned legs, and ball-shaped, wooden decorations here and there gave me a thrill. Those years were a good time for collecting that style of furniture. People were tired of dust-catchers like scalloped mountings and ornamental turrets. If you had the cash, you redecorated your house in the "modern style," chopped up the old furniture and threw the pieces in the stove. The less well-to-do had to be content with removing the ornate attachments and bringing them to the dump.

For me, this was the opportunity of a lifetime. With pounding heart, I rummaged through the rubbish. When I found something beautiful, I had only to bring my mother around. "Oh, Mommy, please...." Then she would nod, "Okay, take it upstairs with the rest of your junk." And radiant with joy, I carried the former showpiece up to the attic where I had set up my treasure chamber.

I would ring our neighbors' doorbells and even try people I did not know. "Don't you have an old gramophone with an old speaker?" Even as a child it was clear to me: a gramophone had to have a horn-shaped speaker. Modern machines didn't interest me at all. I still feel that way; for me, even if it sounds strange, music has to come from a horn.

I am always sensitive to the aura of a clock, a house, or furnishings. Objects put together without love don't do anything for me.

My requests surprised many of the people whose doorbells I rang. Sometimes I would be given something; sometimes I was turned away. People probably thought I was pulling their leg with my constant demands for old objects.

I liked to collect a "useless hodge-podge," as my great-uncle called it. Old keys that didn't fit any lock, particularly whole bunches of rusty keys, were for me something wonderful! I polished them and stuck them into the front pocket of my apron. At that time, aprons for boys, with bands buttoned crossways at the back, were in style and looked just like girls' aprons. That's the reason I was so fond of them.

I still have my mania for aprons. When I got older, they no longer made them for boys. I took my great-uncle by the hand and declared quite matter-of-factly, "Well, then we have to buy aprons made for girls."

My father had his own idea about how a "real" boy should look, and I somehow did not fit that image. I was too handsome, too graceful, with sensitive features and a certain girlish tenderness that gave me a gentle expression.

I liked to put on my mother's school dresses that she had worn before the First World War. They were kept in the attic, neatly folded and packed into chests. Delighted with how they looked on me, I twisted and turned in front of the mirror. My father did not share my delight. When he saw me in such an unmanly outfit, he came at me with a riding crop, ripped the dress off and roared, "You are not a girl! You are going to be a soldier." I was seven or eight at the time.

With terrible regularity, my father used to beat me with a switch. Once, it was too much even for the housekeeper. She tried to calm him down, "Dressing up in his mother's old clothes is just a game for the child!"

At that, my father became even more enraged, "Even if I have to kill him, I'll put a stop to it! I'm in charge of his up-bringing and I can do what I want with him." When the housekeeper objected, he hit her too.

My great-uncle took me to live with him on the first floor of the house in Mahlsdorf. I furnished my room the way a hausfrau would have arranged her parlor around 1890: an elegant Vertikow cabinet in Art Nouveau style, a washstand, a wardrobe, a dainty chest of drawers, the unavoidable regulator clock, and a pier glass with columns. My books were kept in a small cupboard set on a base of turned columns. On one table, I had placed a red plush cloth with a silver-plated receptacle for visiting cards. On a smaller table stood an ornate kerosene lamp. From the junk dealer, I had bought an electrified gas chandelier made of brass with alabaster shades. My little empire!

The pier glass had previously stood between two windows. It had a grooved frame, adorned with arches and columns. On the shelf above, a scalloped ornament, its jambs decorated on either side with wooden globes, was enthroned in Neo-Renaissance style. The frame of the mirror rested on a stand also embellished with lathe-turned pillars.

Not everyone owned a grandfather clock by the end of the nineteenth century. They had to make do with a wall clock or regulator, usually a long glass case with columns on each side, mounted with lathed wooden globes or an eagle made of gypsum that had been dyed to look like walnut. A curved base underneath was decorated with hanging spheres. Inside the case were a pendulum made of brass and a white enameled dial with Roman numerals. I collected such clocks as a child. By now, I have amassed three hundred and sixty-eight of them.

Over the years, my collection began to take up more and more space in my great-uncle's roomy house. I filled the cellar, the attic, and even the adjoining shed with my treasures. With my uncle as an ally, I succeeded in hiding my passion from my father. He never entered those places because they belonged to my great-uncle. Conspiring with me, my uncle would often whisper, "We'll just hide all this from him."

Although during the afternoon I could rummage around in old things to my heart's content, I had to attend school in the morning like everyone else. And—ah—at school things were not much to my taste. Naturally, there were problems with my classmates. Those who aspired to be manly and strong despised me for having golden-blond curls. I was beaten up for wearing hair clips. "You look like a girl," they teased. I was astonished. I had not done anything to them. Why did they want to hurt me? Only later did I understand the invisible wall separating me from most people.

Even worse were the weekly gym classes which didn't interest me at all. Whether we played soccer, broad-jumped into the sand, or climbed poles—it all seemed like nonsense to me. "My God," the energetic but understanding athletic director said, "look at you! You look like a virgin going to a ball. You can't get your legs apart and you certainly don't want to vault over the horse!" He had understood my problem.

Another time, we were practicing soccer at the stadium. Naturally, it was not the round leather ball that fascinated me—my God, that was stupid, kicking the ball back and forth, running around with nervous, sudden moves—but an old train from around 1870 that stood at the edge of the field. In the baggage car without wheels, we changed into our uniforms. Looking around, I could imagine myself on a long journey. I could picture the steam and the locomotive that once upon a time had pulled the car. But then the instructor chased us out and we had to go running after the ball. Soon they realized that I was always kicking the ball in the wrong direction because I had no idea what it was all about. It seemed to me that it didn't matter into which goal I shot the ball as long as it went in. The teacher looked indignant and snapped his fingers to make me come to him. "Do you have fun playing soccer?" he asked. "No," I answered, "I would much rather sit in the beautiful train." And the handsome man with the whistle took pity on me and actually let me have my way.

Being excused from gym meant that my report card read "Unsatisfactory," giving my father further cause to manhandle me twice a year. Not only that, he also tried to make up for my athletic failure with his idea of appropriate educational methods. At Easter time, in 1937 or 1938, he decided to teach me how to swim at the Motzensee. The air was biting cold and the wind whistled around my ears. Definitely not the appropriate weather to go bathing in the lake. A few meters away, a man had made himself comfortable in a tent. My father roared at me, "Undress!" When he saw that I wanted to leave my undershirt and shorts on, his voice again rose, "Take everything off!" As I stood there naked and shivering, my father came close and spitefully asked, "Are you cold?" I had barely said "yes" when he gave me two smacks, right and left, so that blood ran from my mouth and nose. He cut off a birch branch and started to beat me, shouting curses all the time.

The canvas of the tent rustled and the owner stepped resolutely out, admonishing my father in a firm voice, "Don't hit the boy like that."

My father was furious. "I'll do just what I want to him, even if I drown him. That's not your business." Leaving me freezing on the shore, he swam out into the lake. My protector called me into his tent. Sheltered from the wind, I was able to get warm.

There were two beaches at Motzener Tonsee. On the southern shore, the German Federation for Nude Body Culture, a middle-class group of doctors and merchants, disported itself, while on the northern shore swam the communist Priegnitz Organization, which still existed although the Nazis were already in power. In addition to the beach, there was also a four-meter-high diving board on the grounds. My father summoned me up there and ordered, "Today you will learn how to swim. Right now!" From the top, I looked down at the water, terrified because I didn't know how to swim at all, even though my father, whip in hand, had made me practice dry strokes at home. Suddenly it happened. I felt a kick. Plummeting into the water, I could still hear him roaring "Swim!" as I lost consciousness.

I was saved, not by my father, but by a lifeguard who had been standing at the northern end. He pulled me out of the water and dragged me to shore, while my father, unconcerned, observed the scene. After my savior had brought me back to life, he turned on my father, "That was attempted murder!"

"I couldn't care less," barked my father. As far as he was concerned, if I stayed under, well, then I stayed under. Had the lifeguard not been there, I would have "stayed under."

My great-uncle was not only my protector and mentor. I thought of him as my real father. My homeroom teacher was Assistant Principal Dr. Berger. He wore the Nazi party insignia on his lapel and wanted to make us into athletic young men, "Tough as leather, quick as greyhounds, hard as steel." A girlish boy like me, with ringlets, velvet pants and Peter Pan collars on his shirts, was not to his liking. One Wednesday—Hitlerjugend Day—when I was not too eager to put on my Jungvolk uniform, he bellowed, "Hitlerjugend means loyalty."

Without thinking, I answered, "You mean tyranny!"

He swung his cane and struck me. My great-uncle, that gentle soul, accompanied me to school the next day and let my homeroom teacher have it. I had never heard my uncle shout, but that day his voice thundered through all the corridors.

The principal, a dignified gentleman of the old school, who had nothing in common with the Nazis, advised my uncle to send me to private school. There the compulsion to join the Hitlerjugend would not be so rigidly enforced.

I transferred to Dr. Georg Kimpel's Upper School for Boys at Dresdener Strasse 90, third courtyard in the rear, in Luisenstadt. I liked everything about it, even the name of the district, because of my admiration for Queen Luise of Prussia. "Please ring firmly" read the enamel plaque at the entrance to the school. On the stucco façade, suspended from a wrought iron bracket, hung a metal sign with the founding date: 1848. The school, still lost in the era of the Empire, was for me an Eldorado. An old-fashioned clock ticked away in the classroom. An electrified gas chandelier, with green pearls and a white shade, hung from the ceiling. All the furniture dated from about 1890. A picture of the Führer, ubiquitous elsewhere, could not be found here.

My uncle and I sat facing Dr. Kimpel in the director's office. After the formalities of admission were over, the director asked whether I was a member of the Hitlerjugend or the Jungvolk. My uncle wrinkled his brow and said only, "Well, that's just it...." Despite this rather vague answer, Dr. Kimpel seemed to have understood him completely. "You know," he raised both hands guardedly, "my colleagues and I don't care whether the boys are in the Hitlerjugend. It simply means they have a free afternoon without homework and learn nothing." One could, of course, also put it that way.

Even when I was small and didn't know what it was all about, I was repelled by the Nazis. The first time I experienced the brown plague and its messengers firsthand was in the spring of 1933. My uncle had gone shopping with me in Mahlsdorf-Süd. Two brownshirts with arrogant expressions had planted themselves in front of a store that belonged to the Jewish-owned chain Egona. They were trying to keep the customers from entering the store.

My uncle, his old-fashioned Parisian traveling bag that he always used for shopping, in one hand, me on the other, said firmly—and I shall never forget his words—"Please get out of my way."

"Why do you buy from Jews?"

"I'm afraid you'll have to let me decide where I shop."

The two men in uniform looked at one another and let us go past. We went in. I sensed danger in the air. True, the salesgirls were all wearing their aprons and little white caps with "Egona" printed in red, as usual, but the customers were clearly ill at ease. They kept nervously looking towards the entrance. Nobody spoke. After we had safely passed the SA men and were again outside, I asked my uncle, "Who are those nasty men standing there?"

I did not have to wait long for my uncle's answer. "Those are the Nazis—all gangsters!"

I asked myself, *What kind of imbecility are all these flags with swastikas on them and all that rubbish?*

In public school, we all had to put on uniforms and march around whenever the Führer made a speech or when Goebbels, accompanied by a foreign guest, honored Pariser Platz with a visit. Schools were closed and we were marched out. I remember a boiling hot day, at the end of the thirties, when Benito Mussolini or—I could never distinguish among those uniformed clowns, they simply did not interest me—his son-in-law, Italian Secretary of State Count Ciano, happened to be in Berlin and we had to appear before the Hotel Adlon at Pariser Platz in our Jungvolk uniforms.

The smartly trained German youth became sick from the heat. There was not a shade-giving tree or bush in sight; calls for first aid reverberated through the ranks. I spread a timetable over my head to avoid getting a heat stroke—it took hours before the man arrived in his limousine—and I thought of home and how I would really rather be dusting.

Another time, on Wehrmacht Day, we were stationed Unter den Linden and had to cheer the soldiers marching past. Monstrous tanks with huge treads rattled by with the childish faces of steel-helmeted soldiers peeking from the slits. A life-size bomb was displayed on a truck. I jumped back behind the streetlamps and observed a claque of party and state representatives who had probably been commanded to appear, and I almost choked. *Oh my God,* I thought, *what if all this gets out of hand? What's really going on here?* I felt only an instinctive presentiment of danger while everyone around me was overcome with ecstasy.

When I saw pictures of Nazi dignitaries in newspapers, they always seemed grotesque to me. They were men as violent as whiplashes or boot-licking toadies: the bloated smoothness of Himmler's face, who could be mistaken for a bourgeois, small-town teacher at first glance; the cruel simpleton, Foreign Secretary (formerly Champagne Salesman) von Ribbentrop, whose pinched expression was supposed to demonstrate his grave concern for the burdens of state, but whose resemblance to a comic-opera character was apparent to anyone who studied his physiognomy. I detested them through and through, for I knew their type only too well. My father had always struck me as a miniature version of a Nazi bureaucrat. All my loathing for him was unwittingly transferred to the men who were ruling Germany. Even if everybody succumbed to hysteria when Goebbels spoke on the radio, for me it remained vulgar bellowing.

Government is an abstraction. Silently it slinks into our lives and alters our habits, so gradually, it takes years before we notice the effect. So what if crazy specters rule in Wilhelmstrasse? How could that affect Mahlsdorf, where allées of linden trees still exhaled the spirit of the empire? But even here, the brown demon took over. It was the paltry events of daily life that showed me, even at twelve, how much the German people had succumbed to the Führer.

In 1940, the local Nazi big-wigs pushed aside desks and chairs at the Mahlsdorf School at Königsweg to make room for the collecting of metal in honor of the Führer's birthday on April twentieth. Mahlsdorf residents brought in household articles, as well as works of art, made of brass, bronze, copper, zinc, and iron so that the Führer could build even more cannons and bombs. A passionate lover of old clocks and gramophones with horn-shaped speakers, I had, even as a much younger child, tried to rescue them whenever possible. With horror, I saw a man shuffling to the central depot with a huge, perfect brass speaker. Others had already gathered there, pressing bronze figurines, brass candlesticks, metal vases and clocks to their breasts or clutching them under their arms. Upon delivery, everyone received a printed document on which the name of the noble donor was inscribed. On one of the long tables stood an antique anniversary clock, a showpiece. I had never seen anything so beautiful. Under a glass jar, the pendulum, with its shining spheres, moved back and forth between brass columns.

Even those in the crowd who were convinced of the necessity of their actions felt some misgivings. "What a pity to melt down such a clock," someone said with regret. But the supervising Nazi, in a voice filled with awe, told how an old lady had eagerly brought it in. She wanted to donate it to the Führer for the war effort after hearing Dr. Joseph Goebbels' inspiring speech about the metal drive the night before. "After all, nothing is too good for the Führer," he added.

Every word remains fixed in my memory and with the naïve comprehension of a twelve-year-old, I thought, "They are all crazy!" I didn't want to see any more, and ran outside. When I passed by the school a few days later, I saw the brown mob using pitchforks to load the works of art onto a waiting truck. With heavy boots and sledge hammers, they had brutally trampled and destroyed everything beforehand.

During the war, schoolchildren, Jungvolk, and the German Girls Club were always collecting metal and old fabric. One day on my way to school, I looked out the trolley windows at the depot and saw some scrollwork sticking out of the pile of scrap iron. On my way home, I examined the scrap heap more carefully. The ornate leg belonged to a flower stand. Its table top was missing. With great difficulty, I pulled the frame out and scrambled down the heap as quickly as possible. Under threat of harsh punishment, we were forbidden to pilfer this scrap, said to be vital to the war effort. I took the table anyway. Glad to have saved at least one item from being melted down, I found a top to fit the stand when I got home. That table is still standing in my museum at Mahlsdorf.

Chapter 6

AFTER CLASSES, I WANDERED AROUND in the neighborhood of Kimpel's private school. How many things there were to see! One junk shop after another. Soon I knew exactly who had the best gramophones with horns, Edison cylinders, bureaus, ornamental moldings, and Vertikow cabinets. "Vertikow" doesn't come from the French but has its origins in Berlin. Around 1850, a carpenter named Otto Vertikow created these elegant cabinets, which were then manufactured by the millions and still stand in many homes, mostly without their beautiful tops. In September 1941, one of the secondhand shops not far from Schillingsbrücke became my home away from home.

"Furniture Bought and Sold" said the sign on the old building at 148 Köpenicker Strasse, and underneath: "Max Bier, Owner." I went down the steps after one tantalizing glance into the display window: kerosene lamps, picture frames, and porcelain figurines. A bell tinkled. The air smelled musty and comfortable, like old furniture. A slender woman with gray hair and a thin little face with care-worn features came to greet me. There was a stove in one corner and in the center of the basement stood a long table that immediately attracted my attention. On it were spread ashtrays, books, records, cups and saucers; brass chandeliers and gramophones were displayed underneath. Wearing a green apron, Max Bier came from the backroom, where, as I later learned, pictures and frames were stored. Chatting with both of them, I immediately liked them, and they obviously felt the same way about me. I went there almost every day after that. The ambiance of chairs, bureaus, Vertikow cabinets, and portraits of aristocrats in golden frames—oh, it was wonderful!

Like an innkeeper in his comfort-loving way, Max Bier, a good-hearted, occasionally boisterous man of sixty-one years, had indeed once kept a pub in Memel. The Biers had been forced to leave after the First World War and had settled in Berlin. At first, they sold office furniture, but that business had not done well in this impoverished neighborhood, so they switched to dealing in secondhand goods, which provided them with a living.

They quickly realized that I knew about antiques, and I was allowed to make myself useful repairing clocks and furniture. With the money I earned, I was happy to buy old pitchers, lamps, gas chandeliers and eventually, even an Edison phonograph with over five hundred wax cylinders.

"Here is our dear little Levinsohn." Mrs. Bier patted a slim young man on the head. While we shook hands, I examined my counterpart with interest. Despite his seventeen years, he was barely taller than I. He wore a checkered shirt, a gray sweater, and a jacket. His most striking features were his dark and thoughtful, yet frightened eyes, which gazed at me like a shy deer. I immediately took this youth with his reserved air and delicate face into my heart. He was Max Bier's helper, and a Jew.

One day Bier, who was not in the best of health, complained, "We have to move a big estate and little Levinsohn and I can't do it ourselves. Would you like to help us?" Of course I wanted to. From then on, the three of us always set off together. Levinsohn and I did the transporting of smaller lots ourselves. Here I could be myself and feel at ease because in the secondhand shop, I was accepted for what I was—the Biers always called me Lottchen.

One time, I fell in love with a small chest. It was supposed to cost eight marks. Max Bier checked the purchase price, "Well, it cost us only six marks. You can have it for that price. After all, you helped carry it." That evening, I went home with my schoolbag on my shoulders and the chest clutched to my belly. Setting it down every ten minutes, I made it as far as the streetcar to Köpenick.

The conductors knew me by now, and when they saw me arrive with a heavy piece of furniture, they got off to help me. "Well, it must be moving day," they teased, or else they would joke, "Hey, you're breaking child labor laws! We'll have to report you!" Slowly, the train bumped along to Mahlsdorf-Süd. With such deals, I laid the groundwork for my Gründerzeit Museum.

Little Levinsohn and I became fast friends. Whenever an estate needed to be picked up, we pushed and pulled the wagon, piled high with furniture, through the streets. Soon I knew every corner of Berlin. I often bought old books, bargains I obtained at the bookstall on Schillingsbrücke. Eventually, I became friendly with the dealers and was able to buy catalogues about Gründerzeit furniture and architecture very cheaply. I was a constant visitor at a small junk shop called The Secondhand Emperor located across from the church on Stralauer Platz. There, I purchased my first antique wall telephone circa 1900 for five marks, a lot of money for me at the time, money that had to be earned. At times, I had to sell something from my collection, either for space or to obtain more important items.

After school, I couldn't get to Köpenicker Strasse fast enough. I gobbled down the pancakes topped with whortleberry jam that Mrs. Bier had prepared, and then we took off with our cart to pick up wardrobes, chests, and buffets from apartments facing rear courtyards and those that fronted the street, from lower floors and attic rooms. For transporting a piano, I earned ten marks extra.

The Biers treated Levinsohn like their own child. Without paying any attention to Nazi race laws—hardly anyone would have thought of consorting so familiarly with a Jew—we all ate together in the kitchen behind the store. Here, ignoring the race laws was taken for granted.

I arrived as usual at the Biers for lunch on November 14, 1941, but something had happened. Mrs. Bier looked at me with eyes red from weeping. When I asked her what was wrong, she began to cry all over again. Little Levinsohn had not come to work at eight in the morning as usual, and when Max Bier had gone to his apartment, he learned from the neighbors that the whole family had been "called for." We sat there trying to figure out where and why.

"Well," Max Bier said, "they probably need farm workers in Poland and the Jews are being transported there to work the land."

I looked at him questioningly. My stomach contracted and I became almost nauseated with worry. *Would I ever see my Jewish friend again?*

Only then did I realize how much I loved him. From the very beginning, I had been unconsciously aware that his situation was weighing on him and that he was depressed, even though he was by nature cheerful and open. I had sensed his unspoken terror.

My two months with him had passed much too quickly. I hung on his every word; I was on fire to go off with him. He exuded an overpowering aura of sensuality. I have always been drawn to shy youths with gentle dispositions.

When we shook hands, we pressed them together affectionately, a moment longer, as one does when saying hello or good-bye. *Hold on to him, hold on to him,* I thought without realizing it. I wanted to protect him from what he feared. But it didn't work, it didn't work. Tears still come to my eyes when I think of him. If I had only been a little older. I would have hidden him somewhere, done everything for him. I would have pulled him through, that I know. To this very day, I cannot forget Helmut Wolfgang Levinsohn who, as I later learned from a book that recorded his deportation, was murdered with so many others in Minsk.

My love and tenderness always go out to those who have to defend themselves against a hostile world, who are outsiders like myself.

I always take the side of the whores on the street with their dreams; the young boys on the make, already too old for their years; the lesbians and gays; the gypsies—Roma and Sinti—and naturally, the Jews. A strong sense of justice lives deep inside of me, and even more importantly, I feel a kinship with those who live at the edge of society. No one has the right to feel superior to others.

Max Bier had received a registered letter from the finance bureau with the listed assets of a so-called "Jewish bequest." The list contained the price of each piece of furniture in this "bequest." He was supposed to pay the sum to the treasury. *What's happened to the rightful owners?* I asked myself.

Bier was ordered to clear out the place at once. Off the right stairwell of a house on Engel Quay, the apartment had belonged to a married couple. The man was an engineer; the marriage, childless. The nameplate was smeared with red paint that had dried in tear-shaped drops. On the panels, there were scribbled a gallows and the words, "Die Jew." A star of David hung from the cord.

A trembling neighbor, who could barely open her mouth for fear, told us that the Gestapo had appeared at half past one, banged on the door, and when the terrified residents had not opened, they battered down the door with a crowbar and broke the security chain. Like robbers, the Gestapo had stormed into the apartment and beaten the couple as they were pulling themselves out of bed. They were allowed to take only fifty marks, two sandwiches, and whatever they could carry, nothing else.

I can still vividly picture that apartment. The door had been temporarily repaired and sealed when we arrived. On the kitchen table were two half-finished cups of coffee and, next to them, two half-eaten pieces of bread. Directly in front of the plate lay their food ration cards and a notice addressed to Jews, full of prohibitions. Max Bier was bent over the ration cards, "Too much to starve and not enough to live on. What's happening here is an outrage that will take us down with it. Keep your mouth shut and don't say anything at school, otherwise they'll pick us up too and take us to KZ." There it was, for the first time—that ominous word which I was to hear later so often. At the time, I was not sure what horror was implied, but I suspected that it meant being put in prison and never let out.

Inside the apartment, everything was in disorder. Some drawers had been emptied on the floor—those thieves had looked for valuables and found them. To the right, facing the street, lay the bedroom: two bedframes and two Biedermeier cupboards of pale, marbled birch. In one, clothing; in the other, underwear. In the left corner, near the window stood a mahogany bookcase with curved doors, made in the sixties of the last century. The drawer had been pulled out and lay on the rug. Next to it, a small mirrored metal compact. Those wretches had recognized that it was worthless and had heedlessly thrown it on the floor. A thin layer of powder was spread like a veil on the rug and inside the drawer.

All the books were pulled from the shelves and lay, torn to pieces, on the floor. Heine, Goethe, Schiller, and Lessing—shredded and trampled since Jewish books had to make way for Aryan writers. Obviously, the brown-shirted messengers of culture believed Goethe and Schiller to be Jews. I saved a few undamaged Hebrew works and hid them in a closet in Bier's shop. Two books from about 1890, magnificent editions for bibliophiles, were ripped apart. I took the covers home as sad keepsakes. I also kept the bookcase as a silent indictment of the bestial Nazi system which first, robbed Jews of their possessions and then, killed them.

In the autumn of 1945, nobody in the house on Engel Quay could give me any further information about the Jewish couple or their whereabouts. Gone, disposed of, no longer even a memory. From 1946 to 1948, I kept the bookcase at Schloss Friedrichsfelde where I displayed it and told its story. After that, I moved it to the house where I was born, and then, in 1960, to the Gründerzeit Museum. When I discovered that a Jewish museum would again be established in Berlin, I donated the bookcase to the Jewish congregation at Oranienburger Strasse in June of 1986.

Maybe it's my imagination, but each time I see it today, the drawer still seems to retain the delicate fragrance of the powder that the Jewish woman perhaps applied just the day before the Nazi hordes invaded.

Today, if you head from Jannowitz Bridge across Brückenstrasse, then turn left into Köpenicker Strasse, you will see a solitary tree growing on the right side of the street. Nearby, somewhat set back, some modern buildings loom. On that spot, until the bombing shortly before the end of the war, stood apartment houses built in the previous century. The Danzigers lived in one of them. Although Aryan secondhand dealers were not allowed to buy anything from Jews, young, amiable Mrs. Danziger would sometimes appear at Bier's store at twilight. One day she confessed, "We have to part with one piece after another to stay alive."

Soon after that, we were standing in her apartment. Max Bier was buying a three-part mirrored cupboard made in 1880 that I could still sketch today. While Bier and I were taking the piece apart, her elderly grandfather sat in a batwing armchair and stared straight ahead in silence. Knowing that he himself might have acquired the furniture some sixty years ago, it pained me to remove it in front of his eyes. But the aged gentleman had been blind and deaf for some time, and paid no attention to what was going on around him. The next time we went to the apartment, the grandfather had died. "Lucky for him. Who knows what will happen to us," Mrs. Danziger regarded us sadly. We carried off the chair in which the old man, with his cap and snow-white beard, used to sit.

Whenever I arrived from school, I always checked out the display windows of the store first. A few days later, I discovered a photograph, taken in 1901, of a mother and daughter in a molded frame. The price, three marks, was written in chalk on the glass. Mrs. Danziger had brought in her last piece, her last keepsake, early that morning. Later I learned that soon after, the family had been deported and gassed in an extermination camp.

One day, I arrived at the shop somewhat late. I had been kept after school because I couldn't understand mathematics. Max Bier had already gone ahead. Mrs. Bier wrote down the address for me, "Another Jewish bequest," and gave me ten pfennigs for the trolley, Stadtring Line 1. I read the name and address on the streetcar: "Heymann, Prinzenstrasse 99."

The house had been built in the eighties or nineties of the previous century. The façade, entrance, and stairway were decorated with ornate plaster moldings in Neo-Renaissance style. Was the apartment on the first- or second-floor left? The brass plate still read "Heymann," but here also, the door was smeared with red paint. The two ladies, unmarried sisters, were eighty-two and eighty-four. One night, the Gestapo had shoved them, along with some others, onto a truck. Where to? Poland? Where so many people had been killed during the Nazi invasion? *To the labor camps? But what could two such old ladies do in a labor camp?* I toyed with the idea of exchanging nameplates on different apartments, or hiding all the Jews in remote houses, so that the Gestapo couldn't find any of them. But Max Bier reminded me of the many informers, the little Hitlers, the peddlers, those stool pigeons in the house who would make our lives miserable.

The apartment seemed like a house of mourning. We always followed the same routine—collecting possessions and packing them up—like a desecration. I was holding a dark brown regulator clock in my hands. I was struck by the design in the center of the second hand because I had never seen one like it on a regulator before: a star of David.

About twenty years later, I was called to an auction of household goods in the Stralauer Allée. Except for a wall clock, everything had been sold. When I examined it more carefully, I realized it was the Heymann clock. The later owner must have bought it from Max Bier during the war.

"Dr. Wongtschowski, be assured of your fatherland's eternal gratitude," Max Bier said bitterly as he discovered the medals that had been awarded to the doctor for his service in the First World War. We had been ordered to go to Köpenicker Strasse 6, corner Pfuelstrasse. According to other people in the building, Dr. Wongtschowski and his wife had been "called for." Over and over, you heard the harmless phrase, "called for." The words sprang readily to the mouths of neighbors, as if the Wongtschowskis had been called for and taken to a little party by dear friends. Only this time, they had been "called for" to be murdered.

Everything had been left as if the next patient might enter at any moment. A desk with a top circa 1895, originally polished walnut but now painted white; a white cupboard for medicines and instruments; next to that, a chaise lounge. The insignia of an officer in the Kaiser's army were lying in a drawer. The medal for having been wounded and the Iron Cross did not seem to interest the Gestapo. As I stood there looking at the Cross, Bier said, "Take it and honor it as a memorial to Dr. Wongtschowski." Torn documents and a book of poems, whose pages had been shredded, littered the floor. Its tough linen binding, decorated with silver ornaments and the title *Poesie*, had survived. On the title page, I deciphered two inscriptions, "Bianca Pniower, 1891," later, Dr. Wongtschowski's wife, and "Ruth Wongtschowski, 1911," his daughter.

In 1988, after twenty-seven years, I was able to go back to West Berlin, to Köpenicker Strasse, in remembrance. But there was nothing; no tablet points to what had happened there.

Chapter 7

IN 1942, I WAS FORCED TO JOIN the Hitlerjugend since my father had filled out the application form. With a great deal of fanfare the so-called "Münchner certificate" was supposed to be presented to us with bombastic speeches during an assembly at the Berlin-Rummelsburg school. But my friend's certificate and mine had obviously gone astray on the way to Berlin from the "center of the movement." Since I seldom took part in those exercises, my mother received written instructions ordering her to make sure that I participated; otherwise I would be brought before the police. I had to register, and was assigned to the Mahlsdorf Voluntary Duty Unit of the HJ, which we all called the "Forced Duty Unit."

The black sheep from north, south, and central Mahlsdorf were gathered in front of the old manor house. We had special insignia fastened to our uniforms. They didn't interest me much, but they were the cause of a funny experience. One day, as we were presenting ourselves by rank before the troop leader, he fixed each of us with a fierce glare. He stopped in front of me and snorted, "You, standing there like a little saint, under what flag are you enlisted?"

Flag, flag? I tried to remember. *Is anything fluttering in the wind?*

While he was momentarily distracted by something else, the boy next to me whispered, "It's written on your insignia!"

Oh my God, I thought, and squinted at my right shoulder, saw an 18, a line and 124. Just then, the troop leader again turned to me and shouted, "Come on, out with it!"

With my hands held smartly along the side-seams of my pants, I quickly shot back, "18 to 124."

"So, you give me a choice!" he said, his face flushed red as a beet.

Since one was never allowed to just say "yes," I called out promptly, "Jawohl," which at that point seemed like an impertinent come-back. The other boys howled with laughter.

At that, the troop leader, barely able to get the pack under control, roared, "Silence! That's a command!"

He ordered us to go into the house. Once inside, I barely heard his ranting, distracted by the doors with their marvelous moldings and the elegant, simple metal handles on the windows. It was too enchanting! When I finally tore myself away from admiring all that beauty, I had only one desire: to get away from those uniforms and that bellowing ape.

I began to realize the extent of the Nazi horror for the first time in late summer of 1942. On my way to Bier's after school, I turned right off Adalbertstrasse onto Köpenicker Strasse and saw a procession of people: old men and women, as well as young ones, and mothers with children in their arms. They were all carrying small suitcases or bags containing their belongings.

In rows of six, the group, surrounded by uniformed overseers, was being driven over Schillingsbrücke towards the Schlesien train station that is now the main depot. They dragged themselves along, harassed by harsh commands and beatings. *Could these be prisoners of war?* I asked myself. But then I saw the yellow stars of David on their coats and jackets. Like a funeral train, they labored across Schillingsbrücke. Stunned, I arrived at the junk shop and saw Bier standing at the door. Others had also come out of their shops and were staring after the pathetic procession.

Bier signaled for us to go inside. "They are probably transporting them to labor camps, maybe in trains from the Schlesien Station." At that I pictured train compartments, not the cattle cars which were really being used.

"Somebody has to work the idle fields in Poland," Bier suggested. That's what the weekly newsreels were telling the German people.

"Yes, but what about the old? They can't work anymore!" I objected.

"I can't understand it either." Bier became thoughtful.

Mrs. Bier, wearing her usual smock and standing at her accustomed place near the stove, had been listening to our conversation. Suddenly, she pointed her right index finger at us. Her eyes were glittering. "And I tell you, they will murder them all!"

Max Bier, who had been shuffling some papers at his desk, looked up in disbelief, "But Muttchen, they can't possibly murder thousands of people!"

That simple woman with only a grammar school education had instinctively understood what was happening. But we did not take her seriously. After all, she had become a bit strange with the years. Whenever there was a rustling sound somewhere in the basement, she would place a finger on her lips and whisper, "Now they're lowering the listening device down the chimney again." She was slowly succumbing to paranoia.

At six o'clock in the evening, I went to Schlesien Station as usual to take the train to Mahlsdorf. As I waited on the platform, I could see a freight train on the long-distance track. Its engine stood outside the hall, ready to head east. The air vents of the cattle cars had been nailed shut with reinforced wire mesh. I could hear groaning and the cries of children coming from the train. *Is that how people were being taken to Poland?*

Chapter 8

MANY THINGS THAT I DID NOT QUITE UNDERSTAND, but which seemed horrible to me, were happening then. Since I did not comprehend and could not comprehend, until the very end, the terrible catastrophe occurring all around us, I was more focused on the minor tragedy coming to a head at our house.

Even when I was only twelve years old, it was clear to me that the lives of my mother and my younger siblings were in danger. As bad luck would have it, toward the end of 1940, I was supposed to be evacuated to a children's camp in the countryside near Zawisna, which the Nazis had recently renamed "Grenzwiese" because the Polish name displeased them. My entire class had been ordered to go. Afraid that my father might hurt my mother in my absence, I wanted to forestall that threat. Late at night, on the fifth of December, 1940, I furtively crept to my uncle's cupboard and took out his revolver. The cold iron horrified me, but I was determined to end my family's torment once and for all. I stole into the garden and when my father appeared, I aimed and pulled the trigger. Nothing happened. I didn't know to remove the safety catch. My father never noticed anything. A day later, I was on my way.

With a schoolfriend, I went from Grenzwiese to nearby Praszka. Forced to leave their homes, people were hauling their last possessions—chairs, pillows, and bags piled on carts and wagons—and dragging themselves to the part of town that lay beyond the customs station. Wooden posts resembling telephone poles were already neatly rammed into the ground. By our next visit, barbed wire had been strung around the area—the Jews, penned into the ghetto.

What a beautiful building! I had been admiring the synagogue, painted in pale light-blue, divided by four pilasters, flat shafts protruding from the wall, with scrolled capitals and ornate bases. The entrance was cut between two columns, with high narrow decorated windows on either side. A cornice ran around the synagogue, topped by a high tympanum. Rays of light blazed from a gold star of David at the center. My eyes widened in awe.

A few days later, I saw old and young women—it was hard to tell them apart since they were dressed in rags and wore black kerchiefs on their heads—breaking up stones. Horse-drawn wagons rolled up. Armed with iron bars, the women were battering down the walls of the synagogue. *What's going on here?* I could not figure it out.

Again, a few days later, only the left side of the building remained. The Jews, driven by invisible torturers, were razing their own temple with robotic movements. Sad fury, lethargy, and my innocent questions: *Why do they have to destroy the temple? What kind of vileness is this?*

The relationship between my parents had grown worse when I returned from the countryside in September 1941. One evening, my father hit my mother with such violence that he broke her nose.

My mother would never have left Berlin because of the war—the bombing did not frighten her at all—but she took advantage of the evacuation to escape from my father. So it happened that, to our great relief, my mother, my nine-year-old sister, my six-year-old brother and I went to the small town of Bischofsburg in East Prussia on August 10, 1943. We were not fleeing from the bombs, but from our so-called father, a man who did not deserve that title. When we arrived, my mother sobbed, "No matter how the war ends, I am never going back to him." In an ironic twist of fate, it was that horrific war that brought us, for the first time, something like freedom.

We were quartered over the best and largest confectioner's shop in town. Our hosts and we immediately took to each other. In my free time, I was allowed to help in the shop. Many a local lovingly patted my behind. One of them pinched me and winked at me as I bent over the table to make out his bill. What were they thinking? Did they see me as a boy in short, blue corduroy pants, or as a girl with an apron?

From Bischofsburg, I went to visit my godmother, Aunt Luise, who owned a farm nearby. I discovered her old dresses in a baroque wardrobe. She had last worn them in 1895 when she was fifteen. After that, she wore men's garments: boots, jodhpurs, jackets that buttoned to the right, with a Tyrolean hat, and green loden coat. Broad-shouldered and small-hipped, she looked like an estate inspector. Obviously, this was a practical outfit for someone running a farm, but there was also another reason for her style of dressing that I did not suspect at the time: my aunt was a lesbian.

Wearing an ornately trimmed dress with a cinched waist, I was admiring myself in front of the mirror one day, when suddenly the door opened. I could see my aunt's reflection in the mirror as she entered the room. My aunt was a strong-minded person; I was afraid I was really in for it. Instead, she smiled and came toward me. Taking me by the waist, she turned me around and looked me up and down. She seemed amused, "You look really pretty! Tell me, do you like to wear such outfits?" When I nodded shamefacedly, my aunt declared, "You know, nature played a joke on both of us. You should have been a girl, and I, a man." Then, with clanking spurs, she stomped out.

Life moves along in strange ways. Sometimes you put your nose into things without knowing why. One rainy day, I was poking around in my aunt's library, admiring her many books. Aimlessly, I reached into a bookcase, pulled out a book with a gray cover and opened it. Its title was *The Transvestites,* written by a certain Magnus Hirschfeld. *Transvestites? What's that? Certainly not of any interest to me,* I thought.

I was about to replace the book when the next page seemed to turn itself; I read the dedication to my aunt, ending with the words "...respectfully dedicated by the author, Dr. Magnus Hirschfeld, Berlin 1910." Now the book piqued my interest; I began to read. It dealt with the erotic compulsion to cross-dress: men who like to put on colorful summer dresses and women who wear pants and jackets. I was absorbed in the book when my aunt came in. Again, I felt caught. When she asked me what I was reading, I tried to put her off, "It's called *The Transvestites.* I just happened to pick it up."

"Read it carefully," she said, and again surprised me, "It's about both of us."

During the first years of the war, I had begun collecting women's clothing at estate sales. I often found garments I liked and always jumped at the chance to buy anything that fit: blouses, skirts, girdles, and underwear. I shared this passion for women's outfits with Christian, my first friend. Christian looked like a girl and had, even as a child, been a transvestite. We often took baths together, and shared our first erotic experiences.

We were like young lovers, one heart and one soul. At his house, we always put on his mother's dresses and skirts and showed off for each other. One day, with curled hair and ladies' purses under our arms, we hit on the idea of going for a walk along Friedrichstrasse, today called Bolschestrasse, in Friedrichshagen.

There was one thing we had forgotten. During the war, no one under twenty-one was allowed to be on the street after nine o'clock without parental supervision. It was already half past nine as we started out, giggling and in high spirits. Two men in civilian clothes were headed our way; I wanted to wait in an entrance until they passed. But Christian, grown reckless, had no desire to hide. Soon, they were confronting us, "Hey, you two beauties!" They were wearing

Hitlerjugend armbands and wanted us to tell them our names, taking us for two girls out on a lark, teenagers who were trying to get away with something.

Before we realized it, we were cornered and being dragged to a nearby police station. Once there, we were unceremoniously dumped in a cell for refusing to identify ourselves. They threatened to keep us for a month, or to give us a good whipping. We started to feel pretty rotten, with Christian fighting back his tears, and so we gave in and told them our names. The policemen were puzzled, "Come on, girls, stop playing games. Lothar and Christian are boys' names."

I tried to get around it, "Yes, they always call me Lottchen."

"Ah, so that's it!"

"And I'm always called Christine," Christian chimed in. Then they wanted to know our full names and all was in a muddle again. But only for a short time. Abruptly, one of the men on duty reached under Christian's skirt. Shocked, he slapped Christian in the face and called out, "It's really a boy!" Naturally, my examination went the same way. There was a big to-do. Christian's mother was called and bawled out when she appeared. We were warned that if this happened one more time, we would be reported. This time we got off with a sound thrashing administered by the officers. They obviously thought that we two rascals had been playing a joke. Had they suspected the deeper cause, they would surely have reported us as "unnatural" to the Gestapo.

I always hated wearing pants. I only became somewhat reconciled to them as more and more women, particularly after the war, began to wear them.

There was no way I was going to put on my first communion suit. Even though my mother and my uncle tried to talk me into it, saying, "You can't go in short pants, after all," I did not give in. Finally our housekeeper lost patience and announced, "That suit will be put on right now!" As I steadfastly continued to refuse, she ran angrily into the bathroom, got the rug beater, and before I knew it, she put me over her knee and gave me a paddling on the behind. Close to tears, I surrendered to superior force.

"I'd much rather wear a black dress," I brought out in a tear-choked voice.

She regarded the heap of misery in a white shirt, bow-tie, and suit, and had to admit, "True, that would look better on you."

During the war one could only obtain clothing with a ration card. If you purchased a coat, jacket, pants, or socks, whether men's or women's wear, the salespeople would cut a number of points from your card. When I needed a new coat, my uncle warned me on the way to the store, "Be sure you really like the coat you choose. After the points are cut off, it's all over."

The saleslady helped me put on a coat with a belt, which I proceeded to tighten until it could go no further. This made creases wherever you looked. "My child," the saleslady chided, "you have to let the coat hang loose, like this. With the belt that tight, you look like a tied sausage. That's not how it's supposed to fit!"

"But I don't like this style," I answered, after looking at myself in the mirror. "This coat doesn't have a fitted waist and just hangs."

"Coats for boys don't have fitted waistlines," she said with annoyance, "only girls' coats do."

So my uncle and I went to the girls' section, where the salespeople really stared. My uncle was matter-of-fact, "Yes, you've heard correctly. Why don't you check to see if you have a coat that fits him?" They measured my waist and quickly brought a coat from the rack. I looked in the mirror and immediately knew it was the coat for me, with a fitted waistline and soft pleats—exactly how it had to be. Even the saleslady was forced to admit, "Yes, that looks good on you." In short, the coat was bought and the points cut off. As we were leaving, my uncle turned to me, "Let's hope your father doesn't notice, otherwise you'll get a terrible beating." My father never noticed, blind as he was to anything that did not fit into his scheme of things. I don't think he ever realized that I was a girl in a boy's body.

I guess I need to explain that statement to those who understand little or nothing about such an idea. In my soul, I feel like a woman. That does not mean, however, that I am self-conscious about my male sexual organs. I am not a transsexual. On the other hand, I couldn't bear to grow a beard. Even while still in school, I thought, *Sure, you're a boy, but you are really more like a girl.* I had no idea what all that would do to my future, I was so engrossed in being a girl.

But now back to my aunt. Of the several stableboys working on the estate, I liked one in particular. Günther had delicate features, but a masculine body, with broad shoulders and narrow hips. He was supposed to teach me horseback riding. Since it was summertime and I had no proper clothing, I rode out wearing short pants, an obviously unsuitable outfit. My thighs and my behind became painfully chafed.

When we got back, he took me to his room and poured some cold water into an enamel basin. "Okay, now take off your pants."

Overcome with embarrassment, I asked hesitantly, "Take my pants off?"

"Yes," he answered. "Then you can sit in the basin and cool your raw behind."

Shyly, I obeyed. The bath really helped soothe my pain. I became aroused when he insisted on drying me off. We kissed and remained standing in a passionate embrace in the middle of the unlocked room. At that moment, of course, the door opened and in walked my aunt, wanting the stableboy to saddle her horse. Rather than being displeased that he was taking some very private pleasure instead of working, she apologized, "Oops, please forgive me, I didn't know. Just take your time." The door closed. But we hardly took our time, we were too excited. From then on, I spent every free moment with Günther; I was inordinately fond of him.

My aunt was a woman of great understanding, not only about matters of sex, but also politics. She told me about the horrors of the Warsaw ghetto and shared her farsighted judgments about world affairs. "I'm telling you," she began, her face rigid as she sat on the couch, "these criminals who govern us will soon come to a miserable end. But just as too many dogs destroy the hare, we too will suffer. In two years at most, there will be nothing left here. We'll all be poor refugees on the road, and unlike after the First World War, we'll never be able to return to our land."

At fifteen, I thought that a house and its furnishings endured. I didn't dream that one could lose them. Her words disturbed me. Frightened, I asked, "And what happens then?"

"Well," answered my aunt laconically, "some gasoline spilled on the stairs, and the shack goes up in flames. Five years later, everything is in ruins. Trees grow out of the windows."

Such a thought did not calm a collector like me. "And the furniture?" I asked, flabbergasted.

"That's dead matter. It doesn't hurt it to burn. We have to save the animals, that's the important thing."

I had a different idea going around in my head. I wanted to save the beautiful objects in my aunt's house, too. Without her knowledge, I consulted a moving firm to find out how much it would cost to transport all her furniture to an empty barn near Berlin. My aunt read the first items on the list that I had quickly put together—a chest, mirror, vertikow, grandfather clock—and glancing ahead at the next few pages, on which, of course, Gründerzeit furniture was listed, she gave me an amused look. "Darling, you're emptying my entire house. What are we going to sit on? The milking stool?" She laughed heartily. When I assured her that I would pay the moving costs, my resolution seemed to impress her, and the rescue was eventually carried out, with her money.

That was September 1943. Today, I rejoice that thanks to my "madness," her drawing room, mirrors, and chandelier, phonographs, clocks, gramophones, and Edison cylinders have made their roundabout way from the barn near Motzenseebad to Schloss Friedrichsfelde, and are now in my Gründerzeit Museum. Some splendid baroque cabinets I left behind. Although they had neither columns, globes, nor scalloped decorations, they were definitely worth more than all the Gründerzeit junk put together. But that was of no interest to me. I always obeyed my feelings.

On our arrival in Bischofsburg, I had not been able to hide my unhappiness from my aunt. Gradually, I began to tell her about the tyrannical despot at home in Mahlsdorf. She was furious, "If your father ever hits your mother again, smash a chair and strike him with the leg until he shows no sign of life—promise me that! He must not be allowed to live; otherwise he will kill you all." She tightened her grip on the crop she had used earlier that morning to tame some wild horses that the grooms had been afraid to approach. I would swear, had my father been in the room, she would have beaten him to death.

Good and evil were embodied in my mother and father. One thing I learned at that time: A human life, no matter how long it endures, is short. None of us are perfect, but we must have the courage to fight for justice, contend against injustice and protect others from danger under any circumstance and with all our might, even at the risk of our lives.

I had hung some photographs of my great-uncle over my bed in our room in Bischofsburg. He had died the year before. On December 23, 1943, his eightieth birthday, I was standing at our window, looking down at the courtyard. The snow was coming down in thick flakes. A man, wearing a hat and coat, and carrying a suitcase, was coming around the corner through the white blizzard. With horror I recognized him—it was my father. I quickly discarded my "effeminate" apron. Petrified, I watched the door as my father stormed in. He looked around the room without greeting me. When his glance fell on the pictures of my uncle, he ordered me to take them down at once.

He was on Christmas furlough and staying at the hotel Deutsches Haus in town. We celebrated a deceptively harmonious Christmas Eve with our hosts. During his stay, some kind of discussion took place between my parents at my father's hotel. My mother, having consulted a lawyer in Bischofsburg, categorically insisted that she wanted a divorce. At that, he threatened her, and she returned from the hotel greatly distressed.

When my aunt heard about it, she sent for my father. They had a violent argument. Just at the moment a servant entered to deliver a newly arrived letter on a tray, my father raised his service pistol and said, "Another word and I'll shoot." The servant froze, rooted to the spot. My Aunt Luise also drew her revolver. The safety catch clicked, and she warned him, "At the count of three, you'd better be gone, you lowlife, or I'll shoot. One, two...."

My father had not counted on such audacity and withdrew. He had just closed the folding door, when my aunt counted "three" and pulled the trigger. The bullet went though the wood and lodged in another door across the room. "Too bad I missed him," she said, telling the story later. Even after many years, she was still furious at him.

This unbelievably strong woman was always a friend to me. Her lifetime companion had been killed in a so-called euthanasia program. "She is lost," my aunt sighed softly, when I asked after her friend. She probably didn't tell me too much because she thought I was too sensitive, also because, as she later confided, she was in contact with the Polish underground.

In January 1945, she was leading a group of refugees on wagons and horses from East Prussia to Berlin. The Gauleiter of East Prussia, the "Top Criminal" as my aunt used to call him, had given the order that all such fugitives be stopped and executed. In one of the villages, the local Nazi chief attempted to halt the procession. "If you keep going," he roared at my aunt, "I'll have to shoot you."

"That takes two. One who does the shooting and one who lets herself be shot. And I don't belong in the latter category," my aunt answered, calm and resolute.

The Nazi thought she was joking. Even when my aunt drew out the revolver that she had concealed under her fur coat, he did not take her seriously. As he was undoing his holster strap, my aunt pulled the trigger.

"Take his weapons and throw him over the fence into the deep snow. Next spring, the Poles will find a rotten Nazi there," she told the gaping troop of refugees. She urged the horses forward, and on they went to Berlin.

After the war, she acted as a representative of the Polish government-in-exile in London and traveled to Switzerland and England to meet with her superiors. It was all very hush-hush. She lived in West Berlin for a short time after 1945. When I questioned her about her connections, she would laugh and tap my nose with one finger, "Ah, little Fräulein, you just keep worrying about your furniture. You don't understand a thing about politics. I don't want to get you into trouble—after all, you are living in the Soviet sector."

My aunt was not at all interested in pretty outfits. I, of course, cared a great deal about them. Once, as we were strolling along the Ku'damm, I stopped in front of a shop called The Good Line. There, in the display window, was the most beautiful black skirt made of silk or taffeta. I was wearing a woman's blouse, short corduroy pants, knee socks, and ladies' sandals. "Look at that gorgeous skirt," I sighed, full of longing.

"Well, if you want it, I'll buy it for you," my aunt offered.

I was overjoyed.

We entered the shop. A saleslady approached us, but seemed annoyed at our request. My aunt behaved as though there were nothing out of the ordinary about what we wanted. The saleslady plucked the precious garment from the window. My aunt was encouraging, "Why don't you hold the skirt up against him to see how it fits?" The saleslady nodded at me in a friendly way. Obviously, something had clicked for her. She held the skirt against my waist and guessed that it would fit.

In the dressing room, I quickly tried the skirt on. It fit as though it were made for me. I turned around in front of the large mirror in the showroom. My aunt was enthusiastic, "We're buying it. Leave it on."

Afterwards, as we continued walking arm in arm along the Ku'damm towards Halensee, people must have taken us for a grandfather out with his granddaughter.

My aunt told me that from the first time she sat astride a horse when she was six years old, she knew she was a boy. She confessed this to her father who, without further ado, informed his surprised wife that Luise should really have been called Luis. She was actually called Luis by many people later on, but she also had another nickname: the Administrator.

After the wall went up, I could no longer see her. She went to live in England, and we stayed in touch through a British courier. He was an insignificant-looking, friendly man in his late sixties who brought me her letters in an attaché case. Since my aunt was afraid the letters would be opened at the border, I had to answer them on the reverse side of the page while he waited.

She encouraged me from a distance, "Keep on, and don't let yourself be fooled." I never saw her again. She died in 1976 at the age of ninety-six.

Chapter 9

IN THE THIRD REICH, or what was still left of it in 1944, catastrophe ran its course. Most German cities lay in ruins. In Bischofsburg, where we were staying at the time, my mother received a letter notifying her to make rooms available at our house in Mahlsdorf for people whose homes had been bombed. Thus, at the end of January 1944, I returned to Mahlsdorf to rearrange the furniture and make the house ready for these strangers. My father, who was still living in the house, eyed me with suspicion. A sense of doom pervaded Berlin. None of us knew whether we would still have a roof over our heads or even be alive the next day.

One late February night, with all the windows blacked out against air raids, my father confronted me with a choice: whose side was I on—his or my mother's? Somehow, at that moment, for the first time, I had the courage to stand up to him and throw in his face all the cruelties he had committed over the years. He knocked me down to the floor. Then he got his service revolver and loaded it. "You have one hour to think about it. You have to choose," he bullied, "me over your mother." Otherwise he would "kill me like a mad dog and throw me in the manure pit." Then he would go to East Prussia and "shoot down" my mother, my brother, and my sister. These words still ring in my ears, and chills run up and down my spine when I recall that night and the dread I felt.

He locks me into what had been my great-uncle's bedroom and keeps the key. I sit shivering in my nightshirt on the edge of the bed. In the next room, where my father is lying on the couch, the clock strikes. Thirty minutes have gone by. I'm not afraid to die. But he will also kill my mother. Only I can prevent it. But I have no weapons. I see that the maid, while cleaning up the kitchen which is covered with broken glass after an air raid, has neatly spread the cooking utensils on the floor of my uncle's bedroom. I notice the massive ladle used to stir cake dough. It feels heavy in my hand. I will defend myself with it when my father appears in half an hour. But a few minutes later, I realize that I won't be able to do very much with a piece of wood against my father who is always taking target practice in the cellar with his revolver.

I remember that there is another key to the room. My uncle was a careful man. He had an extra key made for every room in the house. I know where this one is kept. I move to the dressing table and pull out the right drawer. It gleams up at me. Slowly, I turn the key in the lock.

I can make out my father's silhouette on the couch. Faint rays of moonlight illuminate the gun on the chair next to him. I creep forward and cautiously move the chair aside. The thick carpet muffles all sound. I leave the revolver where it is. I don't know how to use it. The clock on the wall strikes the hour. My father stretches out his hand to pick up the cold iron and reaches into empty air. I strike. Once, twice, three times....

It was not, and could not have been, done in the heat of passion. I had resolved to act. I knew there was no other choice. When the police came, I felt free in the knowledge that this monster could no longer hurt my mother. His murder was a kind of preventive "self-defense" to save other lives, and I stand by it, even if there is no legal precedent for such a plea. The brutal abuse to which he had subjected me could never excuse my deed. I felt neither hatred nor a need for revenge, but was forced to circumvent his designs on the lives of my mother, sister, and brother.

The police searched for a motive, but found none, and the court delegated the task to a psychiatrist. Counsel Ernst Unger, a warm-hearted man with large thoughtful eyes, escorted me from juvenile court in Tegel to the neurological clinic in Tübingen, where Dr. Robert Ritter was supposed to examine me. A distant, cold, business-like man, Ritter was also the central figure of a racist "gypsy study" in the Third Reich. "Lothar, please don't talk about the Jews, because Dr. Ritter is a Nazi," Counsel Unger kindly warned me. He was worried I would talk too much.

Ritter, a scintillating star among the armchair generals in the National Socialist government, hit on the idea of studying the genetics of "gypsy bastards" in 1935, and had become an expert in this field in the shortest possible time, much to the delight of Reichsführer of the SS, Heinrich Himmler. By November 1936, he had already been promoted to the post of Director of the Institute of Racial Hygiene in Berlin-Dahlem. He and his colleagues were given the task of rounding up all the gypsies, evaluating them, and selecting those who were racially pure. These would be allowed to survive. Like all such studies under the Nazis, this shaky project was supposed to lend scientific support to their theory of the superior Nordic-Aryan race. The "gypsy bastards" who were automatically considered "anti-social" would eventually follow the Jews to the gas chambers. Not that Ritter was a friend of "racially pure" gypsies. They were to be locked up together and made to suffer further "scientific" experiments like animals in a game preserve. How serious Ritter was about his "scientific" pursuits is shown in the macabre protocol of a meeting of the National Security Leadership Council in the winter of 1941–42: Uncertain as to how the "elimination of the gypsy bastards" was to be accomplished, the gentlemen considered drowning them in the Mediterranean. Ritter spoke out against this solution, indicating that the anthropological study he had undertaken was only two-thirds finished. When the additional year allowed Ritter had passed, Himmler ordered all "racially-mixed" gypsies transported to Auschwitz-Birkenau.

With the "solution to the gypsy problem" almost achieved, Ritter turned to a new area of research: juvenile delinquents or "anti-social" youths. In this category belonged, for example, the young fans of "swing" in Hamburg who loved to dance to that American music. This behavior threw Himmler into such a rage that he ordered brutal measures to be taken. Robert Ritter and his assistant Eva Justin were charged with the criminal and biological examination of these youngsters before they were sent to a concentration camp for the young.

Perhaps influenced by reports of my mother's martyrdom in her marriage, or because of the many positive testimonials from our neighbors, Ritter was exceedingly friendly to me in our conversations. He and his assistant took me to town, to Tübingen Palace and to the movies. He also permitted me to give a brief lecture on the Edison phonograph to the students at the university. All this was part of his observation of me in preparation for writing an expert opinion on my case for the court. In the winter semester of 1944–45, he also offered a presentation entitled "An Exercise in Character Modification of Juvenile Delinquents (with Appropriate Demonstrations)" at Tübingen University. I was, without being aware of it, one of these "demonstrations."

Among the gypsies, Eva Justin was known by another name: Lolitschai, which means "red-haired girl" in Roma. She used to snoop around in the detention camps, asking people, particularly the children, seemingly harmless questions about their relatives. As soon as she got the names of these relatives, they were ordered to report to the Institute, where they encountered a somewhat less benign Lolitschai. If one of these miserable victims could not come up with names of ancestors during the interrogation of his family tree, he was told, "If you don't tell the truth, you will be sent to KZ."

Later, shortly before the end of the war, Eva Justin, with the energetic help of her mentor, bagged a promotion with her "Fates of Segregated Gypsy Children and Their Descendants," a work that makes enthusiastic use of her interrogation experiences under Ritter. I had not believed that a doctoral degree could have blood sticking to it. Around thirty thousand German Roma and Sinti were deprived of their lives for the "scientific enrichment" of Doctors Robert Ritter and Eva Justin.

All those human beings had a place, no matter how pathetic, in this world. There were capable and not so capable people among them. But they all had one thing in common: They laughed and cried, played and worked, thought and felt. Ritter and Justin, who were responsible for the deaths of many of them, did not kill a single one with their own hands. They weren't murderers. Every murderer has a motive, no matter how degraded it is: hatred, jealousy, greed. They probably did not even hate their victims. They were not perpetrators. They were only practicing their profession. They measured heads, took blood, filled out neat forms and tables, and wrote expert opinions which were, in the end, death sentences.

These gruesome "scientists" were not usually devils in human shape, which makes the horror of their actions even more shocking, but—in the case of Eva Justin—even took the form of a beautiful, young, strawberry-blond woman, with a small face and medium-length hair. I can still see her, in a ray of sunlight, as she runs up the stairs of the Tübingen Palace with her briefcase, only to disappear behind the door of the Institute. When she shook my hand, she seemed friendly, looking pretty in her white-trimmed, colorful summer dress, her beautiful legs in medium-heeled open-toed shoes. If she touched me, goodness seemed to emanate from her—she was a personification of the banality of evil, the most disturbing aspect of the Nazi barbarity. That it did not require madness or criminality, but simply obedience, a sense of duty, a diligent desire to serve, and the technical ability to accomplish mass murder, should still terrify us today.

After the end of the war, Ritter denied being an accessory to the extermination of the Roma and Sinti, and like so many others, found forbearing judges. The case brought against Ritter in the court of Frankfurt am Main was dropped in 1950. A higher judgment demanded that Ritter, who had in the meantime risen to administrative adviser in the Adenauer Republic, die at age fifty. Who knows to what position he could have risen had he lived for two more decades?

I spent three weeks at the university clinic in their closed ward. The place swarmed with deranged, mostly older people, who had gone mad because of the horrible bombardment, or because they had lost all of their loved ones in the war. I shared a room with a soldier whose brain had been affected by an advanced case of syphilis. Completely debilitated, he took me for a French whore and chased me around the beds. I rang the emergency bell.

A few days later, he had disappeared. When I asked a nurse what had happened to him, I was told in broad Swabian dialect, "Mariaberch, Reutlingen County, that's where he's gotten to, one injection and he's a goner." The Württemberg hospital, where Robert Ritter and Eva Justin ended up just before the collapse of the Third Reich, also served as a "euthanasia station." Since I was being tested for insanity and getting spinal injections, I was terrified that I, too, would be sent to Mariaberg.

I remember that Ritter asked me whether I had ever had sexual intercourse. I looked at him in astonishment. Sexual intercourse? I had never heard that term. Well, didn't I know what went on between a man and a woman? He tried to explain it to me in medical abstractions, "The male member is the connecting tube to the female..." similar to the way it works for birds—but that didn't interest me. Rather, I felt an aversion to his detailed explanation. Surely my reaction had something to do with the fact that sex was a taboo topic at home.

People readily admit when they are hungry or thirsty, but when they are horny, they don't say anything. Nevertheless, it's a part of life that cannot be denied. As a child, sex was made to seem nasty—"pfui," forbidden, and so forth. Once, I had forgotten to lock the door while masturbating in the bathroom. The servant girl burst in and indignantly asked, "Lothar, just what are you doing?" Obviously the question was unnecessary, since it was quite clear what I was doing. The stupid question made me feel guilty about nothing, nothing at all.

But I had also experienced other reactions—my aunt's, for example, when she surprised me "in flagrante" with the stableboy. What good is moralizing? After all, what is a human being? "The most highly developed two-footed animal, nothing more," my mother used to say. I felt no need to tell Robert Ritter any of this. I didn't answer his questions about my sexuality.

In June of 1944, Counselor Unger came to get me at Tübingen to take me back to the Tegel House of Correction for Juvenile Delinquents. Ernst Unger took me under his wing the way my great-uncle had done earlier. Fate had sent me a fatherly friend, at least for a short time. As we took leave of each other inside the walls of the Tegel institution, I was overwhelmed by how much he had done for me.

My trial was to take place in January 1945. My mother had hired a lawyer. When she came to see me the first time after my deed, we barely spoke—we only looked into each other's eyes and shared one thought: we had finally been freed from a nightmare.

The prison, built in the previous century in the form of a cross, had four wings, with the main office in the center. My cell, number 75, was clean and light, with a view to the south. One day, I was moved to cell 13 on the ground floor. I had a terrible fright, not because of superstition, but because the cell was dilapidated and filthy. I scrounged a pail and brush from the caretaker and scrubbed away, beginning with the windows. Although I now had a proper little room with an arched ceiling, this section faced north and not a ray of sunshine could make its way in. I mourned this loss for only a few days—until a bomb hit the south wing, splinters went flying everywhere, and the youth who occupied cell 75 received a fatal head wound.

Days, weeks, and months followed in monotonous succession. I was worried about my mother. I had no idea how she was doing. Letters, infrequently permitted, were always censored. I brooded over whether I could have found another way to save all of us from my father. But I came to the conclusion that I had done the right thing, and all I could hope for was that the judge would be fair. That the government was being run by force and not law was evident when, a few days before my trial, a recruiter for the Wehrmacht appeared and offered me immediate release if I joined. The prison clergyman, Dr. Poelchau, a straight-forward, honest man, noticed the form lying on my table on one of his visits and warned, "Don't sign anything. That's a command that will take you to heaven." He didn't need to say it. I wouldn't have signed up anyway.

Finally, on a dreary, snowy day in January 1945, my trial before the juvenile court in Moabit began. I have only a foggy memory of the proceedings—I was simply too agitated. After my mother gave her testimony, the presiding judge, an old man with a great deal of understanding, summed up, "In all my years of serving as judge, I have never heard of so horrible a married life as your husband forced you to endure. I feel nothing but pity for your son." After a few days, the trial, from which the press had been barred, came to a conclusion. The court found that I could, after all, have fled from my father instead of killing him. The finding of the court, that I could have jumped from the window of the room, only half a story up, filled me with astonishment then, and still does. Where could I have fled in a Germany destroyed by war, which nobody could simply just leave?

My lawyer had requested an acquittal, but the court sentenced me to four years in a juvenile penitentiary, less time served during the inquiry. My mother was told to submit a plea for clemency after half a year. But things turned out differently.

In February and March, the bombing attacks on Berlin became more and more intense. On my seventeenth birthday, I remember the allied bombers emptying their destructive cargo on the city. Low-flying planes zoomed over the rooftops. A Judgment Day mentality ruled inside the prison. To get into the courtyard, you had to stomp through a sea of broken glass, which had once been the windows of the building. On the twenty-second of April, the Red Army marched into Tegel. Chattering anxiously, the guards roamed the halls. All the prisoners were supposed to be moved to the penitentiary in Plötzensee, but one of the transports had been hit on the way by a bomb.

The Russians were already in Tegel. There were no other green "Minnas" available. A guard brought me to the main office. There, at his place behind a large bell, like the captain of a sinking ship, the director sat, talking on the telephone, even as the bombers roared by so low we could almost feel their draft. Five or six other boys were leaning against the wall, also waiting. The director had my file in his hand. With a disdainful gesture, he told the head guard, "Well done. Dismissed," and he disappeared down the hallway.

Chapter 10

HALF AN HOUR LATER, I stood in the street in front of the prison, amazed at the swarm of people trudging towards the center of town, hauling carts full of luggage, carriages piled with quilts, screaming infants in their arms. I asked one woman how to get to the Tegel train station.

"What do you want to go there for?" she asked, flabbergasted.

"I want to take the S train to Mahlsdorf."

Peals of laughter. "The Tegel train station! Ivan is there! Why in the world do you think we're fleeing?"

Like all the others, I decided to go on foot. At Müllerstrasse in Wedding, low-flying planes attacked again. Expecting other people to be hiding in the cellar, I dashed down some steps into a house. Peering through the wooden slats, I saw only rubbish and the most beautiful scalloped top of a cupboard, probably from the nineties, in perfect shape, with wooden globes edging the sides. *My God, what a beautiful top! It has to be saved! The house will probably be destroyed and the scalloped decorations with it.* Those were my thoughts, while the house shook, bombs whistled outside, and the bombardment became more violent. I admit that it is completely absurd to regret the destruction of a scalloped edge in such a situation, but that's how I am. My desire to keep beautiful objects safe is stronger than any other.

As things seemed to have calmed down a bit, I emerged from the cellar. But soon I heard more low-flying planes. I managed to stumble into the station entrance at Seestrasse. A train's red lamps gleamed below. The dispatcher was standing next to the last car. The ticket taker shouted to me, "Hurry up, this is the last one to town. No more after this!" The U train seemed to have waited just for me. As soon as I got on, it started. I sat on that train, all alone in the world. It stopped at every station, but no one else got on. The cars were clean, their windows still intact. The brass rods shone like gold. It was all very eerie.

I had no idea where to get off. I rode to the center, past Friedrichstrasse and Französische Strasse, left the train and got on another one that had just pulled into the track across the way, which took me back to the station at Französische Strasse. I had in the meantime decided that I knew my way around that area better. The station superintendent extinguished the lights as I left. This had also been the last train.

When I came up, I stopped in horror—only ruins and smoking debris where beautiful houses had once stood. The plaque for the firm of Loeser and Wolff still clung to the corner house on Friedrichstrasse. I ran, as quickly as I could, along Französische Strasse towards Kurstrasse. There, I came under fire and fled into the unlocked entrance of the Reichsbank building.

Instead of safety, another shock awaited me in the vestibule. A handful of SS men were gathered there, and raised their guns as soon as they caught sight of me. "Stop or we shoot," one of them shouted.

Dumbfounded, I made a curtsy and said, "Please excuse me, I only wanted to find refuge from the bombing and I'm leaving right away." Without waiting for an answer, I quickly made myself scarce.

Searching for shelter along the walls of houses and ruins, I came to the municipal palace. A troop of soldiers was marching across the square as the noise of battle swelled to an inferno of bursting shells. I dodged into a protected doorway. Fragmentation bombs were exploding all around me. Cowering in the corner of the portico—I was unable to get the heavy door open in the short time I had—I could hear the screams of the dying. Then, everything was quiet. Just a moment before, I had seen the soldiers marching in step, with their packs, rations, and water bottles; now they lay dead and mangled on the ground. The scene was so horrible I almost fainted.

I raced towards Königstrasse, only to be confronted again by bombardment. In despair, I darted into the entrance of an antique shop whose broken door stood half open, at the corner of Burgstrasse. The store had been laid waste by bomb blasts—furniture was strewn around, straw and duct tape trailed from the ceiling. In this scene of dismal destruction stood an old man of about seventy years. He was standing next to a tall, baroque grandfather clock, and stared at me with horror-stricken eyes. He seemed only to be waiting for the next bomb or shell to kill him. This was not a merchant, a peddler for the sake of earning a living—this was an idealist, a real man: an apparition from the nineteenth century, full of dignity and nobility, perhaps the owner of a noble estate, or an officer from the old Prussian school. Straight as a candle, tall, slim, and white-haired, he stood guard next to the clock. His black suit, which he must have worn when serving customers, was covered with dust. Although his features were now stiffened into a mask, I could still discern the educated, genteel aristocrat in him.

He saw me and did not see me, staring right through me. The windows of the shop were shattered. Smoke from the houses burning across the way blew into the room. But that didn't seem to bother him. He could have gone down into the cellar, but no, he stayed in his shop, that was his duty. I felt like an intruder in his domain.

I had not even noticed him at first. Engrossed by the beauty of the clock, I had started to move towards it. Only then I became aware of him, motionless, to the left of the clock, as though he were already on another spiritual plane. I begged his apology for having burst into his shop. He did not answer, and it seemed to me shock had robbed him of his sanity. That house was completely destroyed after the war. What had happened to the old man? Whenever I pass by that corner, which is a barren waste today, I think of him.

After taking my leave of him with a curtsy, I ran towards the Jannowitz Bridge. The cannons had stopped firing. As if it had been decided that I should be the last one to get over, the fusillade recommenced as soon as I was across the bridge. I had just reached the corner of Köpenicker Strasse when, with an awful crash, the steel arches of the bridge collapsed like cooked spaghetti and plunged into the seething depths.

I wanted to see the Biers, but when I got to their shop, it was closed, so I continued on to Melchiorstrasse, where they lived. Mrs. Bier let me in, and both she and Mr. Bier held my hands in theirs for a long time. I had come home to people who cared; I felt safe, even though the war was raging around us. The Biers made a bed ready for me on the couch in the living room. I slept in my coat, for the window panes had been shattered long ago, and it got cold at night. They slept on the floor in the kitchen. The next morning, I was awakened by the uproar of war. We breakfasted on dry bread and water. That was my first and last night in that living room. Behind the wooden wall, the other half of the house had been destroyed by bombs, and whenever bombs exploded nearby, the partition shook, as if about to collapse. I might have fallen to my death from the second floor. The Biers gave me the key to their shop at Köpenicker Strasse. I had to disappear because children were fighting next to old men, and I didn't have the least inclination to take up arms. I couldn't flee to Mahlsdorf. They would have caught me, put me up against the nearest wall, and shot me. On the other hand, I couldn't cower in the junk shop forever. I hardly had anything left to eat. When I finally left my cellar to go into the streets of Berlin, which seemed a city in its death throes, I almost met my doom.

The sign on the wall of the school at Manteuffelstrasse 7 in Berlin SO 36 read, "Room 6, 34 persons." I had fled there when the fury of the bombardment had increased. I didn't know that since the end of April

1945, the military police, the so-called watchdogs, and gangs of SS were chasing down unarmed old men and boys in just such air-raid shelters.

Children, women, and old men were squatting on stools, chairs, and benches that they had brought, with a knapsack or a small suitcase containing their last possessions wedged among them. With half a loaf of bread wrapped in a towel and an alarm clock under my arm, I had garnered a place among some older women who were bluntly speaking their minds.

"Well, how long will those gangsters hang in there?"

"It's better to come to a terrible end, than to be in terror without an end."

"If only the Russians were here already so this misery would come to an end."

Another woman claimed to have more precise information. "Treptow has been taken by the Russians, and there was fighting at the Schlesien Tor. They're already at the Schlesien train station…but what's happening at the Schillingbridge? Brommybridge is down, and the supply depot in Köpenicker Strasse is under bombardment."

But nobody really knew what was happening.

The thunder of cannons and bombs forced its way in from outside. Suddenly, everyone fell silent. In the hallway, a police raid on able-bodied men of all ages had begun. The Biers had told me that a few days ago old men had been led away and shot or hanged in Manteuffelstrasse with signs around their necks proclaiming, "I am too cowardly to defend my fatherland."

Suddenly, the watchdogs were in front of me; they pulled me from my chair and roared, "Why aren't you carrying a weapon?"

I could only stammer, "What should I do with it?" That was, of course, the dumbest thing I could have said.

They shoved me along the hallway to the rear exit and out into a school yard filled with clouds of smoke and the stench of burning. All four had their guns pointed at me; one of them barked, "Attempted flight is punishable by death!" They were driving me towards the half-demolished wall separating the school yard from the rear court-yard of Köpenicker Strasse 152 where Kirchner, a liquor company, was located. Suddenly, a shot rang out on the other side of the wall, a woman screamed, and then there was silence. After we clambered over broken pieces of wall to the courtyard of the factory, I saw a young woman lying on the ground. Blood was seeping from her blouse. A man in civilian garb was just about to pull her skirt down over her knees. A few meters to the side, the executioner, an SS man, was putting away his gun. Next to the dead woman lay a few bottles that had obviously slipped from her grasp. One bottle had been smashed, and red wine was flowing past her feet towards the rubble.

The woman, like so many others, had taken a few bottles from Kirchner's cellar to trade in for bread. That was enough for the SS officer to shoot her for "plundering."

I saw many deaths in the last days of the war, but this young woman shocked me the most—murdered for a few bottles of wine. My horror and pity and the feeling that I could be of no use made me linger for a few seconds. The SS man had asked my guards something, which in my agitation I didn't understand, and one of them answered harshly, "The little fruit without a weapon is ours. We'll take care of him in the next yard." Was he going to shoot me too? I received a kick in the behind, almost losing my balance. I would have fallen on the bottles next to the dead woman had the two guys at my back not grabbed me. They pushed me through the gateway of the factory into the next courtyard.

"Put the bag down!" was the order. But I convulsively clutched everything more tightly, particularly the clock—if I had to, I would die with it. Besides, it was not a bag; it was a towel. Had they said "Put the towel down," who knows, perhaps I would have obeyed. But to put my beautiful clock and my last crust of bread, everything neatly wrapped in a clean white towel, in the dirt? That offended the neat housewife in me, which by then I had already become. As the voice again threatened, "Put the bag down! That's an order!" I stopped caring; I decided not to obey. I was looking down at the ground because I did not want to look at the gun barrels, and had almost given up all thought of escape, when I saw, as if emerging out of nowhere, a pair of boots and Wehrmacht pants with piping. My glance slid slowly upward. I noticed the eagle with the swastika at the breast—and my terror subsided when I saw the face.

Tired, kind eyes regarded me from a careworn face. In that gray-haired man, I could see the human being, not the uniformed officer. Despite the kindliness, he seemed determined and strong, like someone who says, "I'll do what I want." He was cultured and sensitive, not lower-class. He was the opposite of the four SS-bums, who had planted themselves, guns at the ready, a few meters away. The officer gently pushed my shoulders to the wall. After he looked me over, he asked, "Tell me, are you a boy or girl?"

It had been a long time since my last haircut, and I was wearing sandals and knee socks, short pants, and a ladies' coat, cinched at the waist, which my friends had given me from their secondhand goods.

Since I was almost sentenced to death, I thought, *Oh well, shot as a boy or girl, either way I'm dead.* I answered, "A boy."

That started a regular argument between the officer and my tormentors, who obviously did not want to let anyone challenge their right to their prey. The officer asked my age, and I answered, "Sixteen," having completely forgotten that I had turned seventeen on the eighteenth of March. That saved my life. The officer turned abruptly, angrily stamped his foot, and yelled at the patrol, "We haven't sunk so low that we now shoot school children, you damned filthy beasts!"

Suddenly airplanes rumbled overhead; bombs whistled around us; in the other yard someone shouted, "Take cover!" but it was too late. One detonation followed another, and we could hear cries for help and the groans of the dying. Dust and clouds of dense smoke rolled through the gateway passage. The two watchdogs and the SS bandits disappeared into the dust. The officer helped me up, and I leaned, half fainting, against the wall. But he spoke kindly to me, advising me to quickly run away and hide in a cellar, but not in an air-raid shelter. "The Ivans are already in Treptow. In three or four days, they will be at the Schlesien Tor." His soothing words were interrupted by devastating explosions.

The factory had sustained a direct hit. The roof support and the upper story were disintegrating into chunks of stone and falling to the courtyard in slow motion. The officer shouted, "Run!" and was gone a moment later. Not a second too soon, I sprang through the gateway and was again alone. What would have become of me without this officer, who surely had enough to think about instead of standing by me, when one life more or less didn't matter?

After the dust had lifted, I hurried through the various courtyards to the front building. What a contrast! The window panes were all broken—the bombardment had knocked out even the cardboard inserts—but the houses were still standing, and in the yard, from the trees leafed with the first tender green of spring, sparrows twittered as though there were no war, death, or destruction. But out on Köpenicker Strasse things looked grim. The houses across the way were smoking ruins, the whole street strewn with debris. The guide wires for the streetcar lay like torn spider webs on the embankment.

The bridge to the Schlesien train station was under bombardment. As quickly as I could, I ran over the debris to my lodging in Bier's junk shop at Köpenicker Strasse 148. What a sight! The wooden planks I had so carefully installed to protect the display windows had all been blown out. Using the partially splintered boards, I quickly nailed everything up again. The ironware shop across the way was burning down, and the heat of the flames was creeping closer. I hurried to the Biers' apartment in Melchiorstrasse to let them know. When I told him, Max Bier said bitterly, "Now the Nazis will pay for their crimes, but we will be drawn into the abyss with them." We barely had anything left to eat or drink.

With our last bread coupons, I joined a long snaking line at the bakery in Melchiorstrasse. Bombs were falling in the next street. Suddenly, the baker's crying wife appeared in the door. The back where the baking was done had sustained a direct hit; the baker and his helper had been killed instantly. We all looked at each other. Nobody said a word. Then the shutters rattled down. The bakery was gone.

The bigger Hitlerjungen were often asking me where my weapon was, and since, as I had discovered for myself, it had gotten more and more dangerous to wander around the disintegrating city in the last days of Nazi barbarity, I decided to get a gun at the police station at Wrangelstrasse 20. I would, of course, not fire a single shot unless at a Nazi or the SS. On Wrangelstrasse, too, half-starved people were looting the stores. The boards to replace the broken windows had been carried off long ago for fuel. Starved, I stepped through the display window of a grocery swarming with people. Hoping to find even a few crackers, I stumbled around among the wrecked cupboards. Rotting peas and flour were strewn all over the floor. Nothing that I could eat.

The half-open door at the entrance to the police station hung askew on its hinges. I knocked on a door on the first floor. No one answered. I entered. A man, probably the chief, was sitting at a table, a revolver in front of him. At my request for a weapon, he pointed absentmindedly into the next room. It was eerie. The door to this room was wide open. Splintered glass was strewn over the furniture and floor. Everything seemed to be falling apart. Somehow that calmed me.

Voices were coming from the last room. Since the door was closed, I knocked. Without waiting for a "come in," I entered the room. Five policemen were lounging about. One of them raised a bottle of Schnapps to me, and put it to his mouth. Two bottles were being passed around. All of them, except one, seemed tipsy. Loud laughter greeted my request for a weapon. "Girlie, you're good, but first you have to put on a uniform, the final BDM order." Somebody mumbled something about being "heroic," and I wondered if they had all gone crazy. The sober guy was examining me from head to toe; the whole thing was becoming unpleasant. He pointed with his hand to a corner behind their lockers, "The weapons are over there, all of them from 1914, but there is no ammunition left. You can take one and pretend it's loaded, but I don't advise it. It's all over anyway." I laughed with relief. But soon they were saying, "Hey girlie, you're cute. Stay a while and let's have some fun. And here, you're under police protection." The tipsiest guy staggered towards me, grabbed me around the waist and gave me a kiss. The smell of bad liquor, the uniform—while a house less than a hundred meters away was being bombarded—it all seemed like the end of the world. Without a weapon, I left the room as quickly as possible and ran out of the building.

Back at Köpenicker Strasse—chaos. Soldiers and even SS men barged through the broken door down the steps into the junk shop. They all wanted to get rid of their uniforms and weapons, and get into civilian outfits. But I sent them on, because I realized it might cost me my life if the Russians found uniforms and weapons there. The statue of "Old Fritz" on his horse, standing in the front room of the junk shop, an exact copy of the one Unter den Linden, seemed to be amazed at this voluntary "demilitarization."

The next day, a woman I did not know but who lived nearby, dashed through the broken door of the shop, embraced me and shouted, "They're here, the war is over! They're coming down Köpenicker Strasse; the supply depot is taken; Manteuffel and Wrangelstrasse are swarming with Russians. We're free at last!" Then she rushed away, leaving me standing there, bewildered. But after a few minutes, I realized that what I had yearned for had finally happened. I didn't believe the Nazi propaganda about Russian atrocities and that the Russians would kill all of us. But not all my fears were gone. The SS was still in charge at the Engel embankment.

On the afternoon of April 26, 1945, heavy Russian tanks clattered towards the center of the city, followed by infantry troops. Wagons pulled by horses made their laborious way over the rubble-strewn Köpenicker Strasse. Russian soldiers, in their earth-colored uniforms, were unloading rolls of cables; I wondered whether they were planning to install electricity, until I saw one of the soldiers in the next house open a wooden box and listen into it: field telephones were being installed with frantic speed. The shooting had shifted more and more towards Jannowitz Bridge, and since I was curious, I stood half-hidden in the doorway of the junk shop. More and more soldiers were moving past. Some called out to me and laughed. I didn't understand any of it, but I laughed and waved back. As the shooting became louder, I withdrew into the kitchen in back of the shop. A Soviet officer, his translator, and a few soldiers came into the cellar to advise me to leave the battle zone since the SS might still be hiding in the area and might raze everything.

All this time, hordes of people with baby carriages and carts had been moving towards Treptow, laboriously trying to rescue their last possessions from the inferno. I joined the silent crowd. The shooting got so bad behind Manteuffelstrasse that I sought shelter in the large vestibule of the Provisions Bureau. It was crowded with Russian women who had been carried off by the Nazis as forced labor and who were now free.

The day after I left the junk shop, scattered Nazis set the house on fire with flamethrowers. A young woman lived half a flight up. During my last visit, I had tried to make her see that she would be safer and warmer in the cellar. But she didn't want to move. She was afraid the house might collapse and she would be buried in the cellar. I shall never forget the picture of her standing at the window, her child in her arms, a dusty mahogany desk behind her. I wonder what happened to her....

The treasure of valuable Jewish and Hebrew books that Max Bier and I had painstakingly saved was burned by the SS hoodlums and their flamethrowers. We had watched over these works—a serious crime in those days—to safeguard them for another era. Since there was always the danger of house searches or examinations, I had placed a cardboard sign labeled "Old Paper" on the pile of books. But all my effort was in vain. I could not protect them from the flames.

A mangled trolley car barred the way to the main train station at Schlesien Tor. I could get past Köpenicker Strasse by going left, but there, tongues of flames were spewing from a house. I looked around—nobody near or far. I was the last one. I was afraid that the façade might come crashing down. But how else could I get past? With the collar of my coat pulled over my head, I ran through the fiery oven. Past the Schlesien Tor was the Treptower Highway, today the Puschkinallée. That road was clear. We had survived. People were resting on the cement base of the iron fence that ringed the villas where the staff of the Red Army was quartered. There was a hurried coming and going of messengers, officers, and ordinary soldiers. On the sidewalk, Red Army men were distributing army-ration bread. I was given a slice. I had long ago eaten my last crust of bread. Only the clock remained wrapped in my towel—although I couldn't eat it, I always knew what time it was. I sat down on the wall, ate my slice of bread and breathed a sigh of relief.

Many streetcars with boarded-up windows had been left standing on two tracks in front of the Treptow train station. As it was getting dark, I thought of spending the night in one of them, but it was a hopeless endeavor. The cars were overflowing with people. Some had even tried to make themselves comfortable on the steps. I moved on towards the Treptow streetcar station in search of shelter. In the empty yard, I actually discovered a railcar, one of the well-appointed old cars from the time of the First World War, with a skylight on top, and its interior paneled with mahogany. I pulled the cord, and the brass bells tolled melodiously across the deserted train station. I curled up in one of the seats and slept the unburdened sleep of youth—until someone touched my arm.

I was terrified as I came to, blinking into the glare of a flashlight, with soldiers' guns aimed at me. SS? No, they were wearing the less threatening earth-colored uniforms. I couldn't understand their gibberish, but guessed they wanted me to stand up and be searched for weapons. The control squad left the car with lowered guns. In high spirits, I vacated my asylum.

The noise of war had quieted down, but heavy trucks bringing soldiers and fresh supplies continued rolling towards the center of town. Clumsily, one soldier came riding by on a shaky bicycle, threw it down on the ground a few meters from me and disappeared. I examined it more carefully. No, he would definitely not come back for that bicycle. It did have two wheels, handlebars, and a seat, but tires, mud-guards, and a hand brake were missing. I returned to the streetcar with my find, and to catch some more sleep. But at five-thirty, the night came to a definite end—the thunder of cannons tore me out of my slumber. I took a few test spins on my bicycle around the trolley. All went well. A patrol stopped me, examined the bicycle, but let me go with the comment "No good." But now where to? I couldn't go back to the junk shop. A barrier had been erected at the very beginning of Schlesien Strasse, and only military vehicles were allowed through. I turned around, shakily pedaling east towards the Treptower Highway. I wanted to go home to Mahlsdorf.

Surrounded by refugees and supply trucks for the Red Army, I pedaled towards Köpenick. As I passed the ruins of the Jewish synagogue that had been destroyed in 1938, I thought, *Finally, this bestial criminal system has come to an end.*

On the gable of the Jewish Old Age Home on Mahlsdorfer Strasse, a Star of David again bloomed above the columns. In 1942, the Nazis had "called for" the Jewish inhabitants, and had deported and gassed them. The Hitlerjugend had taken the house over; soon, oil paintings robbed from the old Jews hung along the corridors and in the rooms of the officials. The Star of David was hidden by the HJ emblem.

In the fifties, a scaffolding was raised at the entrance to the old age home, the Star of David was removed and replaced by a cement block. That a memorial tablet should be placed on this house and, of course, the Star of David be returned to the gable has not, even in the DDR era, occurred to the council of this district nor to the Division of Education to this very day.

As I started out on the Schlesien Bridge on the morning of April 27, 1945, the hands on my old clock pointed to six. At twelve noon, I walked through the garden gate of the house where I was born in Mahlsdorf—free from air-raid alarms, bombs, and shelling—to begin a new life.

Chapter 11

THE HOUSE WAS FILLED, at least four to a room, with refugees and people whose homes had been bombed. Laundry lines stretched like rays of light from the chandeliers to the walls. I moved into the cellar. In May, a Red Army troop occupied the house; within one hour, all the inhabitants, allowed to take only the barest necessities with them, were evicted. I alighted in an attic room nearby. Now I had a dry place to stay, but nothing to eat. My life was saved by the occupation forces.

I soon established contact with the soldiers in our house, and was allowed to go into our garden. Eventually, they permitted me to make myself comfortable in two rooms in the stable with our furniture that had been stored, undamaged, in the cellar. I now had "a room and kitchen."

Even when the sun was shining outside, the Russians left the chandeliers on all day in some of the rooms. All the radios were tuned to the transmitter in Moscow. Little Father Stalin's speeches reverberated throughout the house. The fuses kept burning out. The orderlies were constantly coming to me in the stable and gesticulating wildly with their hands. "It doesn't work, it doesn't work!" They dashed back into the house, with me right behind them. The fuses were soon used up. Since no new ones could be procured, I was constantly repairing the old ones with thin wiring.

"It doesn't work" could also mean something else. It could mean that the cast iron, funnel-shaped, enameled toilet bowl from the year 1914 was completely stopped up and threatening to overflow. Everything was soon repaired with a rubber plunger, while the orderly stood by, filled with admiration. As a way of thanking me, he would invite me into the dining room, pour out a huge water glass of vodka for me and make a toast.

I don't drink at all, since I have always found the odor of alcohol offensively pungent. But I did not want to hurt the feelings of the good-natured orderly. When he turned around, I would spill the contents of the glass out the window into the garden...may the flowers forgive me.

Seeing the empty glass, his face would light up from ear to ear, and showing his white teeth, he would pour another glass to the brim and call out, "Drink, drink!" Surely he meant well, but it would not have gone down well. And so I waited for the moment when he would roll up something for me to eat in an old *Pravda*, with Comrade Stalin gazing sternly from the title page, and I would once again water the flowers with vodka.

At first, I was forbidden to go into the cellar on my own. The soldiers were afraid that I might blow up the house. When they began to trust me, I was allowed to move into the whitewashed rooms again. Completely in my element, I made myself at home in my little apartment, cleaned the windows, and hung up little curtains.

At the time, I was living on nettle soup, unripe berries, and water. If the soldiers had not given me a few things to eat here and there, I simply would have starved. I was glad when something "didn't work."

At first, Soviet soldiers had looting rights, and in order for them to carry off whatever they needed, it was forbidden to lock houses or apartments. Women and girls did well to hide if they wanted to avoid being raped. Whenever Russians were on the march at night, the residents would beat pot covers together to sound the alarm. Along with the cry, "Commander, commander!" the system worked pretty well, and the soldiers, usually drunk, would move on. The metal din did a good job of revealing the street where the military could be found. I don't want to whitewash things. There were excesses committed by Russian soldiers, particularly towards women and girls, but it all ended rather quickly because the draconian punishment for rape frightened most of the perpetrators away. When my mother was threatened by a man in the Red Army, a mounted officer rode up and prepared to shoot him on the spot. Her pleas dissuaded the officer from his intention, and the soldier thanked my mother profusely.

On a hot, sunny day in July 1945, my mother, sister, and brother returned, and we fell into each other's arms. How much we had to tell each other! They had been evacuated on the last train out of Bischofsburg to Kunersdorf in the Erzgebirge in October 1944, just ahead of the advancing Red Army. With many adventures, they made their way on freight trains, horse carts—and on foot—to get as far as Schöneweide at the end of the war. There, they stowed some of their goods and made their way to Mahlsdorf with a hand-drawn cart.

A month later, our occupiers were busy with travel preparations. The red velvet rug that dated back to the emperor's time was particularly irresistible to the soldiers. They decorated the back rest of the officer's car with the rug from my uncle's parlor, and hung curtains, cut down to fit, at the side windows, as if longing for a little comfort after such a terrible war. A young man, sitting on the supply wagon, was plucking at the strings of my mother's guitar. The soldiers were toasting each other with old beer glasses filled with vodka. Waving and singing sad melodies, the column proceeded to its Potsdam garrison.

We did not have to wait long for the next troop. A German-speaking officer, with whom I liked to chat, told me, "Hitler no good, Stalin also no good." He considered both the red and the brown dictatorships to be tyrannies.

Many houses and fences displayed red flags in the summer of 1945. Some of the flags had a dark, round spot in the center where the swastika had been ripped off by new adherents. But there were also convinced communists who had fought the Nazis even in the Weimar Republic. They now hoped for better times.

Soon we were again free to live in all the rooms of our house, but life was hard. My mother weighed only eighty pounds and suffered from starvation edema; my siblings kept crying because they were so hungry. One day, in despair, my mother took me aside in the kitchen, "We have just traded my last pieces of jewelry for food. We can't pay our gas and electric bills, and we can't eat the house. I don't know what to do. There is nothing left for us to do except to turn on the gas." I had to do something—after all, I was now the provider for the family.

As soon as the trolley started to run, I went to the Biers' second-hand shop to try and get work. But even as the trolley was squealing along Köpenicker Strasse, I saw that the house where the shop had been was now in ruins. I found grieving Mrs. Bier in emergency quarters; her apartment had been bombed. Her husband had died of starvation two weeks before. I often think of his prophetic words, "We also shall be dragged into the abyss with them."

But I did not despair. I attached notices to the trees in Mahlsdorf offering chests, tables, chairs, bedsteads, washstands, wall mirrors, records, gramophones, and kitchen utensils, since I had plenty of those. And people really did come to buy. They paid very little, a chair covered in leather for five marks, a Vertikow cabinet for twenty-five, a wall mirror and bedstead for fifty marks—but after all, nobody had much money.

I hit on the idea of opening a secondhand shop but the gods had set the Bureau of Trade against making that plan a reality. I went to the town hall in Lichtenberg, my first contact with a German bureau since the war. My proposal was denied for the unassailable reason that second-hand shops were no longer needed. *The same stalls, only different pigs,*

I thought. I could not foresee that this would go on for another forty years.

The unemployment bureau sent me to a builder's carpentry shop. There I stood, in the bitter cold and snow—it had since turned winter—inappropriately dressed in my narrow-waisted ladies' coat and shoes that were falling apart. I was supposed to drag a large stack of resinous planks from the yard into the shop. In a short while, the foreman noticed my hands and knees were blue with cold. In the chief's waiting room, where I could finally warm myself, I could hear him on the telephone with someone at the unemployment bureau, "What kind of starving girl did you send me? She's half dead from the cold and needs a warm workplace, right in front of the stove. What I need is a strong workman with a ration card I and not such a sissy with a ration card V for housewives. So, I'm gonna send her right back to you.

"What, that's a boy? You can't fool me—an old Berliner like me can tell the difference."

Obviously not always!

I traded that job for one in a Mahlsdorf bicycle shop. Fritz Heppert, the owner, soon sent me to his wife in the kitchen. "Lottchen, you are too slow for this work. You can't earn any money here. You'll be better off in the kitchen." Without any doubt he was right about that, and his wife was very happy with her new maid.

"Pier glass and secondhand household goods for sale." The notice nailed to a tree in our neighborhood intrigued me; before long, I found myself in Mahlsdorf-Süd at the given address, Steinstrasse 31. The windows had Art Nouveau railings with the initials FZ engraved on them. The cast iron relief on the gable of the house depicted a locomotive with a tall chimney. I wondered who lived there. A marble sign answered my question. "Franz Zimmermann, Locomotive Engineer to His Royal Prussian Highness, Retired."

But Franz Zimmermann was no longer alive. His son and daughter-in-law were now living in the villa and wanted to get rid of most of the furnishings. Zimmermann had heaped up various objects throughout his life—from trinkets and kitsch to rare objects and works of art—more out of an inclination toward than an understanding of art. I undertook the liquidation, a fascinating project, but not very lucrative, particularly since I bought many Gründerzeit pieces myself.

The house and its inhabitants had an exciting story behind them. The high windows and the folding doors, still there today, came from the Berlin Palais Unter den Linden of Count Reedern. The original owner of the Mahlsdorf villa had served as chief steward to this nobleman. When the palace was destroyed in 1907 by the hotelier Adlon to build his famous hotel on that property, the steward had saved some pieces of the old construction.

Thus, not only the windows and the folding doors, but also four sandstone statues that had graced the ramparts of the palace ended up, via roundabout ways, in Mahlsdorf. Zimmermann placed them as decorations in his front yard, without being aware of their value. Eager to obtain these statues, a collector of old sculptures drove his carriage all over Mahlsdorf until he found them in Zimmermann's front yard. He paid as much for the sculptures as the steward's house had cost him to build.

Old Zimmermann was a monarchist. He hated the Nazis and didn't have much love for the Russians either. Thus, when the Red troops occupied Mahlsdorf, he got an ancient uniform of the old Prussian kingdom out of the closet and placed himself, unloaded gun at the ready, on the top step, "The Russians shall cross this threshold over my dead body." At sight of the old gentleman in his museum-piece outfit and his ancient weapon—in his loyalty to the emperor he had even attached the bayonet—the soldiers could not hold their laughter. They disarmed him and promised not to loot his house. Everything remained untouched. Only two small events angered the old locomotive engineer. During the search, one Red Army soldier shat in the base of the grandfather clock in the dining room, while another one peed in the tureen nearby.

The whole house seemed like a museum as I entered it, a year after those unappetizing events. The wife of the engineer, a former schoolteacher, had whole-heartedly shared his collector's passion.

In 1946, I learned that the palace in Friedrichsfelde was to be torn down. As soon as the Russians cleared out, vandals took over the baroque palace and, like vultures and hyenas at a dead animal, were tearing out boards, rafters, doors, and parts of the banister for firewood. Almost three hundred years of history does not count when someone here and now needs firewood to warm himself or to cook a meal.

But I felt differently. With its architecture and banquet hall, the beautiful palace that had impressed me since childhood was to be torn down? That shocked me. *What a shame,* I thought, and went to the Bureau of Estate Management. Somehow, this mad decision had to be overturned.

No, there was no way to prevent the planned demolition. I was told that funds had already been allotted. I don't need to stress how difficult it is, particularly in Germany, to declare decisions of the state null and void once funds have been allotted and red tape has taken over. As a rule, the officials look at you as if you were an anarchist wanting to destroy their sacred order. My attempt to salvage the palace—which surely would be doomed from the start today—succeeded in the chaotic days of 1946, when every regulation was carried to its ridiculous extreme.

In one of the side rooms of the Bureau of Property Management, an old white-haired lady was pecking away at a typewriter. Emmy Schneider, the former secretary to the owner of the palace, Sigesmund von Treskow, asked, "So, you want to take possession of the palace?" Then she turned to the director, "Mr. Schubert, let's give him the palace. We can make better use of the money by building three silos on the farm."

"What a good idea," he agreed. Herr Schubert examined me, nevertheless, from top to bottom with bemused reservation. His astonished glance fell on my short pants. "Do you have the money to rebuild a palace?"

"No," I answered, "I don't have any money at all, but I do have two hands."

Chapter 12

I WALK TO THE PALACE through an allée of plane trees. A caryatid—one of those wonderful female statues—that previously held a lamp, now lightless, greets me from the pond. Crossing the ramp added in 1908 during the reconstruction of the palace, I make my way into the entrance hall: imposing, mighty. I admire the wonderful oak stairway that ascends to the second floor. To the right is a sandstone fireplace from the seventeenth century. Tapestry-like fabrics, frayed and torn, cover the walls. Through the skylight, rays of sunshine fall on the coffered ceiling. I approach the stairway with its curved, baroque balustrade.

Through a double-winged folding door, I enter a room to the right. It is hung with blue tapestry and is completely empty. The oak shutters, supported on the original handmade rods from 1695, close flawlessly. In the next room, light-winged classical paintings…a poem from the year 1800. Brass rods run along the molding where paintings, suspended from bronze loops, contrast with the white-gold wallpaper. The parquet floor, old and good, exudes solidity, as does the white-tiled stove.

Back into the entrance hall, and from there, into the northern ground-floor reception room. Yellow wallpaper and a porcelain oven in each corner, decorated with sculptures of children. Classical cornices. Oak panels, parquet, windows with bayonet catches. Wooden frames from the Biedermeier era have been inserted into the mullions. The cast iron railings of a stairway, leading from the front pavilion into the garden, end in candelabras.

Back into the entrance hall. To the left, a room with red wallpaper. Parquet and oak wainscoting. An obtuse angle, black and white marble flagstones set into the parquet floor tell their own story: here the people who lived in the palace warmed themselves at the fireplace.

From the ground-floor hall into the former drawing room. Wooden beams divide the wall covered in wine-red velvet. A massive carved chimney, narrow and towering. The fireplace, flanked by two caryatids supporting the magnificent mantelpiece, is pure classicism.

Standing in the entrance hall, I see that the upper story has rhythmically-spaced brackets around the stucco molding under the cove. The ellipse of the ceiling is framed in an oval of painted garlands that continue down the cove.

Up the oaken stairway to the second floor. Between the first and second landing, a section of the balustrade along the wall is missing. It's been chopped up by refugees to feed hungry stoves.

At the top, I enter the grand ballroom through the center door. Four pairs of columns with Corinthian capitals support the ceiling. Mirrors between the pilasters on the walls reflect light coming in from the windows opposite them. The ellipse of the ceiling is enclosed in flower-entwined lattice work and a pale summer sky with small, plump, dimpled clouds. The four corners of the cove are ornamented with frescoes: a celebration of flags, lances, and drums.

East of the ballroom: the cotton-damask room. The fabric is in shreds. Under the covering, wooden wainscoting had been painted green and divided into panels. The painted ceiling, in fan-like sections, is overwhelmingly beautiful. A wing of the door is missing—torn-out for more firewood.

The room behind the library, ruined; the ceiling collapsed; wet mildewed rubble covering the floor. Here, in 1772, Prince Louis Ferdinand von Preussen was born, and in 1779, his brother August.

When I viewed the palace for the first time, the glory of past centuries was crumbled, destroyed, carried off, but the old charm, somewhat tainted, remained.

The verdict regarding Prussian militaristic traditions had been announced at the Potsdam conference of the victorious nations at Schloss Cäcilienhof in the summer of 1945. The constitutional division of Prussia by the allied command was only a postscript to the death certificate that had been drawn-up. In the Soviet zone, they went to work with alacrity, "legal proceedings against Junker estates" also applied to the ruined stones of aristocratic heritage.

Schloss Friedrichsfelde, not of Prussian origin, but erected in 1695 by Benjamin Raule, a Dutchman, as a small, villa-like summer house instead of a hunting lodge, was in terrible condition when I took over. All the windows were broken, the shutters demolished, the doors missing, and the roof was full of holes from the bombing.

To begin repairs, I gathered roof tiles from barns about to be destroyed, after getting permission from the farmers. With keys I had filed myself, I was able to lock the front door. I nailed strong planks across the door to the terrace for a little more security against the Russian soldiers marauding through the area and whose "visit" I feared. Only then did I start to really get everything in order.

I worked mainly at night, climbing around on the roof in the pale moonlight, working my way through the rooms, screwing, hammering, and drilling. During the day, people sauntered through the park; at night, lovers arranged rendezvous or, weather permitting, more. In the nearby village, people were whispering to each other with a conspiratorial air that something strange was going on at the palace. Since I walked through the rooms with a candlestick and made knocking noises with my repair work, people suspected the palace was haunted.

I moved in with my uncle's Art Nouveau furniture; next came a living room and a workroom, which I still own today; then a small dining room with a breakfront decorated with columns, and furniture from my aunt's salon. And, of course, an immense number of clocks, gramophones, automated music players, chandeliers, paintings, and furniture. With these pieces, I eventually fully furnished five rooms. Since the cold was unbearable on the upper floors, I moved into a warm little room in the cellar of the palace, as befits a servant girl.

I had gotten three rooms ready. Wearing a kerchief and apron, I was cleaning the blue salon with the windows wide open. The music box with its twelve little bells was playing a song that could be heard in the park. A bunch of people had gathered in front of the window. When the piece was over, someone called out, "Hey, that was nice. Can you play it again?"

"Come on in and look at the box; the door is open," I answered. Suddenly I was surrounded by twenty-five people, eagerly looking around. I was perplexed. *This could be tricky,* I thought. No panes in the windows, nothing restored, and sparrows making free with the upper floors. Besides, I had never given a tour to strangers. I wound up the music box again and hoped it would satisfy everybody.

As the last notes died away, they applauded, and one of them asked to see the other rooms of the palace. We ascended the old stairway and entered the ballroom on the first floor. That the handles were missing on the doors, the panes were not yet set into the window frames, and bats were suspended, head down, from the stucco cornices didn't seem to bother anyone. I told them about the history of the grand ballroom and the fates of the owners. At the end of the little tour, one of the group asked, "That was very interesting. How can we make a donation?" I didn't know what to say.

In the entrance hall, a majolica vase was displayed on the shelf of a pier glass. "That vase over there has a big belly, let's throw something into it," an older woman suggested. And indeed, they all lined up, the coins jingled, and on emptying the vase, I found that it contained eighty-six marks. In those days, before the currency revaluation, one could buy a loaf of bread for that amount. *Not much,* I thought, *but pretty good for telling a bit of a story.*

The next Sunday at a quarter to eleven, immediately after the service in the nearby parish, visitors again appeared at the palace. I drew up a sign and hung it on the latch with a string. "Guided tours through the palace every Sunday at eleven and twelve o'clock. At other hours by appointment." I still maintain that schedule today in my Gründerzeit Museum.

At first, I lived in the ruins alone. After a few months, farm workers and refugees came and asked if they could move in with me and how much the rent was. "Nothing," I answered, "but you have to get panes for whatever rooms you want to use." Glass was still being rationed, and you could never get as much as you needed. Old X-ray plates were obtained from the hospital nearby, washed and cut to size. From a junk shop at the Schlesien train station, I bought old, worthless pictures, removed the frames, cut the glass down and set it into the lower parts of the windows. I nailed cardboard into the upper sections and filled the space in between with leaves for insulation, so that not even snowstorms could tamper with my construction.

The refugees and I were like a family. We would sit together in the evening. Sometimes, I played a record and we danced to it.

But in the spring of 1948, two officious gentlemen from the trust company suddenly appeared at the door. Standing in the entrance hall, they summarily informed us that we were to vacate the house. All of the families had already been assigned living quarters. That's how things were then. "Do you have any furniture?" I asked the people who had shared the house with me, and of whom I had grown very fond. "We moved in with a cart, and we'll move out with one," was the answer. I didn't allow that to happen, but gave some of my collection to the families. That way, we were all helped: I had to leave the palace within three days and could not take everything with me. Without much ado, the construction workers put my furniture in the garden, and I carted everything with a horse and wagon to Mahlsdorf. Naturally, a piece here and there was missing each time I came back from a trip, but what could I do?

Next, with feminine cunning, I tried to entice the district magistrate of Bernau out of the idea of destroying Schloss Dahlwitz. With two horse-drawn carts full of furniture, I moved into the neoclassical structure, built by the Jewish architect Friedrich Hitzig in 1854.

"You've got to get out of here. You don't have a chance of setting up a museum here. We don't want it, and we don't need it. The palace is a Junker estate and must be torn down. Basta!" the mayor declared, after throwing a disgusted look at my collection. Without inquiring about it, he probably thought it was furniture from some palace and thus an abomination from some aristocratic hell.

There was no talking to that man; I might as well have talked to the wall. Instead, I went to talk to the magistrate's office in Bernau, a little northeast of Berlin—the bureau truly in charge—and bothered the magistrate until he agreed to inspect the palace with me.

When he caught sight of the coat of arms on the terrace, he was ready to turn back, declaring, "We are going to destroy all these Junker palaces; there's no way of getting around that."

My objections to his plan were vehemently socialist, "Comrade, all of it now belongs to us, the people. It was taken away from the Junkers long ago, and we could make this palace into something useful for workers, a children's home for example."

At the prospect of a children's home, he nodded thoughtfully and said, thinking out loud, "Well, we really do need a children's home."

Soon boys and girls were romping around in Dalwitzer Palace. The classical stucco work was of course knocked off. When I go past on my bicycle these days, I stop a moment to walk thoughtfully around the palace and wish it well.

Chapter 13

BEGINNING IN 1945, I often wore women's clothes to go about the neighborhood. Winters, of course, I wore pants and a long coat, but when the weather permitted, I wore a dress.

Wearing women's clothing, I naturally took a chance on being roughly accosted by Russian soldiers. But I was in luck. One day, some Russian soldiers had already pulled my skirt up and were about to rape me, but when they didn't find what they were looking for, they broke out in raucous laughter. One gave me a slap on the behind, and that was it—it could have gone much worse!

The people of Mahlsdorf who knew me from childhood just good-naturedly shrugged their shoulders, "Gee, it's funny the way he wears those old-fashioned dresses and only runs around with men, never women. Is he queer?" That was all.

Little Christine, my old classmate with whom I had run into the arms of a Hitlerjugend patrol when we were fourteen and both in drag, was not so lucky. She liked to flirt and prance around in pumps and summer dresses, wear falsies and a brassiere, and go to gay hang-outs. After the war, as she was parading around the Friedrichshagen train station near the men's toilets, she fell into the hands of five Russians who obviously thought her some kind of German wonder-woman. "Come Frau, sleep Mädchen, come away, away." Christine shook her blond mane, but the Russians grabbed her by the arm. She tore herself loose, and with Comrade Russki in full pursuit, ran across a field towards the outdoor theater. Tripping over a tree stump, she flew up in the air and fell down hard. Her purse rolled heaven knows where, but she was on her feet right away. In such a moment, a slut thinks of lipstick and compact, not about running away. The five Russians dragged Christine into a dark corner on a park bench and went to work on her. Man or woman, it made no difference to them when it came down to it.

Little Christine came crying to me in pain. I took her to a doctor. He shook his head but found she had only an infection.

Christine worked many years as a secretary and was accepted by her colleagues. She was given a pension in 1980 and moved to West Berlin to follow the man of her dreams.

Watchmaker or furniture dealer? My mother wondered what I should become. My great-uncle had discouraged me from the watchmaker's trade. "Watchmaker? To sit all day in a shop with a magnifying glass in your eye? When you grow old, you can't see properly anymore," he worried.

When it became fashionable to make smooth, bulky furniture in the thirties, I lost the desire to spend my life among pieces that were not from the Gründerzeit. Having become a kind of servant girl after the war, I was taken aside by my mother, "This can't go on. You have to learn a real profession." Since the songs on my Edison records were often in English, I became interested in that language. I took some courses and passed an interpreter exam in 1949. Thus I learned a "real profession" before my education as a museum conservator began.

The winter of 1948–49 was barbarously cold. We traded the unheated rooms of the language school, where our fingers got so stiff we could barely write, for the grand apartment of our fellow-student Mechthild. Every pupil had to bring one briquette to each lesson so that the small emergency stove could be lit. We also kept our coats on. Mechthild's best friend was Uschi Dressler, daughter of August-Wilhelm Dressler, the painter. Restless as a whirlwind and colorfully dressed, she was a perfect Bohemian, and in accordance with the cliché about artists, she never had any money in her pocket. With roguish eyes shining from her pretty oval face, she would greet me with the exaggerated gestures of an actress, "Ah, Lotharchen!"

August-Wilhelm Dressler—not very tall, thick-set, gray-haired—regarded my bare legs with interest as I appeared in short pants in his atelier to repair the clock on his mantel. Pictures of plump naked women were displayed on easels. Because of his expressionist paintings, his works had been proscribed by the Nazis. "Wouldn't you like to pose for me at ten marks an hour?" he suggested.

After my initial dismay, I began to like the idea. I might be shy, but I was no prude. And the money was tempting. Records cost only fifty pfennigs, a blouse, three marks fifty; a beautiful new ladies' skirt, five marks. For eight marks fifty, I could look nice all summer.

"I am handsome." The phrase went through my head as I gazed into the huge, rounded mirror while posing naked, and the students in Dressler's art class were busy painting my leg bent around a stool. If I got bored, I admired the beautiful mullioned windows and the Biedermeier furniture of the atelier.

PHOTOGRAPHS

With Mother and Great-Uncle

My mother, Gretchen Berfelde, born Gaupp

In the garden of my birthplace in Mahlsdorf-Süd

Ten years old

"I look like an ox adorned for a festival" (Whitsuntide)
—Aunt Luise, again in women's clothing after fifty-five years

Great-Uncle Josef Brauner

In the workroom with my great-uncle's furniture

Friend and collector, Alfred Kirschner

Storeroom in the Gründerzeit Museum with the remnants of the original collection

The whipping stand from the Mulackritze

The Mulackritze and the last innkeepers, Minna and Alfred Mahlich

With Werner Pfullmann

The air-raid shelter in Kreuzberger

Camp where children were evacuated during wartime in Sawisna/Grenzwiese

Friedrichsfelde Palace

The Homosexual Community Interest Group of Berlin on an outing

The mansion in Mahlsdorf

In the Gründerzeit Museum

Great-Uncle Josef Brauner

The State's Service Cross

Chapter 14

I AM ESSENTIALLY A LONER and always have been. Keeping myself occupied with housekeeping, furniture, and more recently, puttering about in my museum, has almost always been enough for me. But only almost—sexuality doesn't let itself be suppressed; after all, why should it be?

In 1949, I went for the first time to a "teahouse," a public toilet known as a place to meet men. Someone had encouraged me to go to one in the park where a lot of men hung around. "Go pick one up!"

At that time, you could not advertise, and a gay subculture in bars did not exist. So what was there to do if you didn't want to live like a monk? And I didn't want to do that under any circumstance.

With very mixed emotions, I walked into the toilet at the Bellevue subway station. I really just wanted to look around, but the atmosphere got me going. Notices were scribbled on the tiles—who was looking for whom and for what. That's when I first realized that, here, you could also meet someone who might become a friend.

"My God, what a sweet creature you are!" The older man who had entered the toilet regarded me affably. We sat down on a bench outside and talked to one another. It has always been important to me to find out what sort of person I'm dealing with, and if I can trust him. Whether the men were young or old, handsome or not so handsome, was never important to me. Because of my feminine reserve and modesty—I didn't go with everyone by any means—I perhaps avoided certain dangers.

I had a wonderful night with my first teahouse acquaintance, and the next morning after breakfast, he squeezed my arm. "Sweetheart, I've never had someone as adorable as you. You're the first one who didn't ask for cigarettes or money right away."

It was shortly after the currency reform, and he really wanted to give me twenty marks. Astonished, I rejected his offering. "No, no, you keep it. It gave me pleasure too." He seemed perplexed to have found someone who was willing to spend the night with him out of friendship and love.

When I was twenty-two, I got to know a very masculine girl who had rough features like a boxer and fascinated me somehow. Though she didn't particularly arouse me, I liked the way she ran around the neighborhood in short leather pants. One day, this buxom young woman jokingly threatened, "You're like a girl. One of these days, I'll get your skirt up and rape you." I didn't take her seriously, but a few days later when we were alone in her parents' apartment, she grabbed me, threw me on the bed, fiddled with my short pants and pulled them down. Shoes flew into the corner. She performed an insane ride on top of me, squeezed my breasts, and gripped my arms so that I felt as if I were the woman and she, the man.

With a passive woman on top or under me, I could not have started anything, but with sexually active Herta, as the gay-loving Amazon was called, it worked. Afterwards, I was overcome with an overwhelming terror, "Oh God, what if she has my baby?"

How dumb I still was became clear a week later, when sitting in her parents' home, she looked at me and asked, "Say, Lotharchen, you look so sad. What's the matter?"

"Oh, Herta, I'm looking at your belly. It seems to me it's already a little bigger than last week." I really thought she was pregnant!

Herta almost choked laughing. "Lotharchen, get this straight—that takes three-quarters of a year. Besides, I can't get pregnant anymore." I was bewildered until she marched over to a chest, opened a drawer, and returned with a medical certificate which proved her contention.

That was my first excursion into the heterosexual world, and it was rather frightening.

In the early fifties, I became acquainted with a painter. His landscapes were awarded to the victorious jockeys who raced on the Hoppegarten track. Since the prizes were also displayed in showcases at the Hoppegarten, he needed picture frames. And I had plenty of those.

At that time, a former officer in the emperor's army, Herbert von Zitzenau, previously an active rider himself, was hired to do the weighing and judging at Hoppegarten. One day, he stopped in front of the showcases and said to the painter, "Where do you get such beautiful old frames? That kind of frame doesn't exist anymore."

"A young man in Mahlsdorf collects this kind of stuff," the artist answered.

Intrigued, Zitzenau decided at once, "I must get to know him. I also like to have old things around me."

We were invited to tea. I was all excited: Herr von Zitzenau, a gentleman rider with a villa in Karlshorst—right away, I naturally thought of a Gründerzeit villa with at least twelve rooms. I made myself as attractive as possible: short pants, sky-blue blouse, and my hair nicely curled. With the train station some distance behind us, I got a funny feeling. The surroundings were getting more and more ordinary. The sidewalk did not lead to a wrought-iron fence, but turned to gravel instead. Here, there could be nothing great...good-bye, Gründerzeit villa. Finally we were standing in front of a small garden with a modest single-family house, built in 1926. No outside stairway, nor anything else of grandeur. The wire fence was so rusted, one had the impression that only the entwined wild lilac held it together. There was a simple Prussian mailbox made of wood with a scratched nameplate. At our ring, a one-armed man, old, but tall and strong, appeared at the side door. He greeted us amiably but without ceremony. I was somewhat disappointed and embarrassed as well.

He told stories about the past and showed the house, only a part of which he now lived in. Most of the rooms were rented out. I noticed the filthy carpets and runners, and Zitzenau, discomfited—my glance had not escaped him—said, "Yes, I've got a singer and an actress living here, but you mustn't look at the floor. The women are all very beautiful, but none of them clean."

The dignified gentleman had in the meantime won my sympathy. He had hit on my passion for cleaning, and I offered myself as household help. He couldn't pay very well since he received only a small pension, and the state didn't give him a pfennig for his war disability; but for a small stipend and payment in kind, all the "rubbish" lying around in the storeroom, old chandeliers, glasses, and pictures, I began to work for him as a maid. In a trice, the rooms were absolutely clean.

My main income came from working at the Märkische Museum. For many years, beginning in 1949, I used to help remove the rubble from the museum, at first as a volunteer. One day the museum director, Professor Dr. Walter Stengel, whom I greatly admired, took me aside. "You know, you're born for the museum. In three years, you'll be conservator." And so it happened. I put the storage rooms in order and restored musical machines. I took clocks apart and put them together again as the old clockmaker in Köpenick had taught me when I was ten years old. "You can save the three marks fifty for the repair," he had greeted me, when I had come to him with a broken regulator. "Just come here, young man, I'll show you how it works. There is nothing really wrong with your clock. All you need to do is replace the spring for the pendulum, clean and oil it." No sooner said than done. That clock still runs today.

In the meantime, the Märkische Museum had entered into a firm verbal agreement with me. Until 1971, that is. Invited to a party, I threw on some fancy dress, put on a wig and had a great time. A good-natured man from the theater section of the museum was also at the party, and some time later, during morning break, he told his colleagues about his "exotic" experience, "Our Lottchen looked so cute at the party in her wig, blue dress, and necklace."

Although intended as harmless, the remark had unpleasant results. Another colleague denounced me. A few days later, right after I came to work, I was summoned to the office of the acting director, SED member Manfred Maurer. He was sitting behind his desk and said, with such malice in his voice that I immediately mistrusted him, "Colleague Berfelde, have a seat."

I knew something was wrong, that they were up to no good. Actually, they should have been grateful to me since I often worked much longer than I needed to, washing windows and cleaning up.

"Last weekend you allegedly appeared at a party in drag." He paused briefly before bringing out the phrase "in drag," obviously struggling for breath in his outrage. One could clearly hear the disgust in his voice. He didn't just say the ominous phrase, he vomited it.

I was fuming inside—just what business of the museum was my private life?—but outwardly, I remained friendly. "Yes, you heard correctly. I wore a sky-blue dress, a gold-blond wig, and a string of pearls around my throat, and I had a wonderful time."

Comrade Maurer coughed nervously. "Oh, yes, the new laws since 1969…but you must not forget that you are working in a state institution."

"You know," I continued glibly, "whether I run around the streets in pants or a dress makes no difference. Anyone who isn't a fool can see from a hundred yards away that I am really a woman."

I wasn't fired at once, oh no. They used more subtle means to get rid of me. They came after me by mocking me with the title "Goose-girl of Mahlsdorf" because nights I used to take care of pigs, ducks, and geese at a farm.

Then, the administration forbade me to give guided tours in short pants because some women had complained about my appearance. "Does the young man who plays the music for us get so little money that he can't afford long pants?" It was all nonsense, of course. The secretary told me that such complaints were never made. Such narrow-minded fault-finding would have been absurd at a time when short pants were in style and women were running around all over the place in hot pants with their buttocks jiggling. I decided, *Okay, if that's how they want it, let them wallow in their own shit.*

My word-of-honor contract usually ran for a year. I waited until March 31, 1971, and, as I suspected, it was not renewed.

While there were some good people working in the music machine section of the museum, they had only a limited idea of how to care for and repair the delicate mechanisms. A pneumatically operated orchestrion that imitated twenty-eight instruments, with the mechanism for all of the instruments and a spool of notes in its housing, was the centerpiece of the collection. As if it wanted revenge itself on the narrow-minded administration of the museum, it gave up its ghost half a year after I was let go. Now the gentlemen from the museum came snivelling to me, babbling about a contract as supervisor; they were naturally only bent on getting their main attraction going again cheaply. I refused, and they had no choice but to get two mechanics from Köpenick. At a loss about what to do, the two examined the orchestrion, and somewhat crushed admitted, "We can repair the mechanical parts, but not the pneumatic mechanism." The museum had to import an organ builder from Leipzig, who took the entire machine apart. Three men worked on it for half a year. Altogether, the repair devoured eleven thousand marks. Had I done it—and I can't deny myself the pleasure of laughing at them—the whole repair job of equalizing the pressure and cleaning and replacing the valves would have cost sixty marks. *Serves you right, you idiots,* I thought.

But back to my adventure with the gentleman rider Zitzenau from Karlshorst. Like many women, I wanted to be seduced. And Zitzenau, part cavalier of the old school, part libertine with the jocular, salty voice of a Prussian officer, did it. One day, a storm was ominously approaching. To my annoyance, I had just cleaned the windows. I stood there, staring through the shiny panes. A thunderstorm was moving towards us from the west like a black wall. Zitzenau thought it wiser for me to stay, since I couldn't possibly make it to the trolley station in time. Undecided, I was still looking out the window when the bicyclists started pulling their capes over their heads and the first downpour began. Suddenly, Zitzenau was behind me, reaching between my buttocks. An erotic lightning bolt went through me; what followed was a classical seduction.

Thus began our intimate friendship. That he was over sixty didn't bother me at all. I've always had a weakness for older men, and I felt safe with him. What else could a woman want? We frequently went to the Hoppegarten racetrack together, where the musicians would play my favorite songs at my request—the "Amboss-Polka" or the waltz "Over the Waves" by Juventino Rosas. The audience, enthusiastically applauding the musicians, never suspected that the blond, merry young lady in the old-fashioned summer dress was really a young man.

Dresses make the lady if one has the figure, and I had it. Once a "real" woman jealously asked me where I had my dresses made. Leaning against the parapet of the music pavilion, I readily answered, "At a junk shop." She laughed heartily and wagged her finger at me, as if I had tried to put one over on her. Nonplused, I watched her leave in a huff.

In 1957, Zitzenau suffered a stroke, and lying in Sankt Hedwig Hospital, he was under no illusions about his end, "I'll never leave here." I tried to cheer him up, but he waved me off. A few days later he died. We had been together for five years. Not physically faithful, no. Zitzenau had regularly encouraged me to get to know other men.

I again frequented public toilets and got to know a few men here and there. I trusted some of them enough to enter into friendships with them that lasted until, if they happened to live in the West, the wall went up.

Chapter 15

I WENT TO A GAY BAR for the first time with some friends from West Berlin since I never would have dared to go alone. They were encouraging, "Lottchen, there's nothing to be afraid of." I put on a dress and minced along. A railing guarded the few steps down to the pub. We rang and were admitted. The interior was unexpected: an old brown sideboard on wheels from the turn of the century, blackened with smoke, with a flat counter in front for the bar. On the wall to the left hung a picture of Berlin as it had been—a row of houses, gaslights, city gates. An ancient brass lamp was suspended by a hook from the stucco-decorated ceiling. Everything hinted at 1900, another era. But on the worn-out chairs, their cushions so faded that their original colors could no longer be determined, life was focused on the here and now. Half-naked young men, in fancy evening dresses or in enchanting, almost transparent, flimsy garments, were sitting on the laps of their admirers and chattering away. In this topsy-turvy turmoil, there was one stable rock: the hostess, wearing a striking motorcycle outfit.

"Hey, cut it out," she bossed in a heavy Berlin dialect and cuffed one of the guests who had been talking nonsense, then stomped back behind the bar.

She's got everything under control, I thought, as I stood in the oldest scenic pub at Görlitzer train station: Elli's Beerhall.

Elli, uninhibited and resolute, examined me carefully as I shyly ordered some juice. "Hey, sweetheart, you've really dolled yourself up," she teased.

I liked her rough masculine style, and she must have liked my feminine reserve. When I visited the bar the next time, in a peasant dress for a change, she picked me up, put me on the bar and laughingly said, "You're my ornamental doll."

The toilets were located in a small back room, and when the transvestites in their dresses tried to turn the knob to the men's toilet, some smart aleck would call out, "Other door!"

"A little bit of 'bi' doesn't hurt," smirked Elli and grabbed me under my skirt. Although she was a lesbian—her friend worked there as a barmaid—Elli wasn't too rigid about it, as I know from experience.... Once in a while, little sado-masochistic parties were held in the back room. If anyone was put over the table and Elli made ready to let him have a few, we knew: Elli doesn't just crack the whip, she makes sure it burns. Most of the time, however, we indulged in more harmless pleasures.

One weekend, since Elli had just bought a new record player, a dance was advertised. A huge crowd of gays and lesbians packed the bar, but just as the dance was supposed to start, the thing gave out. Elli stormed at me, "Come on, Lottchen, have a look at it, you know all about musical machinery." When I picked up the cover and saw all the wires, lines, bulbs and heaven knows what else, I threw up my hands. "Sorry, this makes as much sense to me as clockwork to a cow. It's no go." The whole dance was about to be scuttled, when someone suggested, "Say, Lottchen, can't you bring your gramophone instead?" And that was it—somebody drove his car up, and off we went to bring the gramophone and records.

The huge brass horn blasted music from the bar. People were hopping around all over the place, and I gave my first performance. I knew the lyrics by heart, and whenever the old records were too scratchy, I would join in. From then on, wearing a dress or short corduroy pants, dark blue or black, bought cheaply in Neukölln for six marks at Hertie's, I would stand by the gramophone every weekend, while all around me romped gays in jeans, just then coming into fashion, or in leather "Bayern look" shorts. During intermission, Elli would bring me juice and something to eat. Sometimes she would even give me belts and shoes as presents. "Look at that, see how nice it goes with your dress."

In 1961, overnight, it was all over. "For the prevention of hostile activities by the aggressive and militaristic powers of West Germany and West Berlin," the decree of the DDR Council stated on August 12, 1961, "strict controls at the border between the Deutschen Demokratischen Republic and the Western Sector of the Borough of Berlin shall be established as is customary among sovereign states."

It had been decided in Moscow to hinder the "draining away" of people from such a vital puppet state by simply locking in the inhabitants. Although we had accepted the founding of the DDR with a shrug of the shoulders—at that time it didn't touch us at all—the consequences were now becoming clear. Subtly phrased, the degree made us the final prisoners of war, the final sacrifice to National Socialism without which there never would have been a wall with watchtowers and barbed wire—a fact easily forgotten.

People were having a wild discussion the next day on the front platform of the trolley car.

"Hey, they are really securing the border, driving their tanks up and down, and building a wall."

"Oh, it won't be so bad," another one put in, "that business with the wall won't last fourteen days."

"Not even that," hazarded a third.

"Don't fool yourself, the Russians, not Ulbricht, are behind this," I contradicted him. And from their anxious faces I could tell that I was only saying what they suspected but did not want to believe.

"Yes," an older man agreed, "the wall could last one year, or ten years."

"No, that's not possible. Think of all the actors, artists, doctors, who work in this sick ward...it wouldn't last long...."

"You'd be surprised," prophesied the streetcar conductor. "It can last a long time if the western powers don't intervene. And I don't think they will." He was right.

In 1988, after twenty-seven years, I stood sniffing memories in Elli's Beerhall. "Here I played the gramophone," I explained to Moni, who now managed the place. Elli had died the year before. "When was that?" Moni asked. I felt as though it had been yesterday. "That must have been long ago," she drawled, and made a gesture as though to wave the thought away. It made me realize that, indeed, almost three decades had gone by since then.

I asked about my friends of that long-gone era—after Claudetta, a transvestite with whom I had passed many free and easy hours. "He's over seventy and lives in the old age home on Blücherstrasse. But he usually comes around on Sunday."

The following Sunday, early in the evening, I was standing next to her at the bar. "Look who's coming in," Moni whispered to me. An old, white-haired little man in eyeglasses shuffled to his familiar place in the corner, sat down heavily on the sofa and ordered beer and cognac. "Claudetta," Moni called out, "Who do you think is sitting here at the bar?" Claudetta raised his head, his glance searching the room. "Lottchen, you?" Happy, and sad at the same time, I had at least met one of my old friends again.

That was the saddest chapter for me, as I started my journey "abroad" to Kreuzberg, Tempelhof, Charlottenburg, Neukölln, and Spandau. Besides traveling to places I remembered—Max Bier's second-hand shop, Dr. Wongtschowski's apartment, the school, and air-raid shelter at Manteuffelstrasse 7—I also wanted to see the people whom I had been fond of. Claudetta was the only one still alive.

But back to the fifties. Max Palmowsky, my love after the death of Zitzenau, comes to mind. I was sorting keys at Ludwig's hardware shop on Schloss-strasse at the corner of Seelingstrasse in Charlottenburg when Max came in. He collected antiques and bric-a-brac, and was a regular customer. The next time I appeared at the shop, Ludwig whispered to me, "Hey you, Max is really interested in you. He'd like to invite you to tea." Max had a tiny, but tastefully furnished apartment in the rear. He definitely did not want to just drink tea with me. I had barely sat down next to him on the Biedermeier sofa when he began to show me pictures of naked men, original prints of French workmanship, some of them from the last century. At the time, that was something new to me.

Max was bisexual, tall, slim, dark-haired and exactly my type. Around fifty years old, he had an air of fatherly calm. When I was with him, I felt I had reached a secure port. I didn't mind that he also went for women. Why should I? But he certainly had a weakness for buxom women, big machines, with asses like dray horses.

A matron just to his taste lived in Mahlsdorf. She was looking for a potent, slim, dark-haired man. Although I acted as a kind of matchmaker, I did warn him, "She is so fat, she'll be too much for you."

"That's okay," Max answered with a glint in his eye. "Get that woman for me." He invited her for coffee, with me in attendance. "I am no prude," the Valkyrie roared, "and before we get going, I'd like to see the two of you in action."

I had reservations. Both of us in front of this woman? Max liked the idea, but wanted to draw her into our game and lasciviously demanded that she also get undressed. She submitted without objection—I didn't even want to look. Such a fat woman with that kind of behind and huge breasts would have killed any desire on my part. Max, on the other hand, was very aroused, and against all the rules of the game, they got it on. I felt no jealousy because I was not sexually attracted to her at all. For me, that woman was a complete zero.

I formed an erotic companionship with Max which lasted until the wall was built. We wrote to each other regularly after that. In 1967, a letter of mine was returned as undeliverable. Addressee not found. I could not even find Max's grave. I guess that is to be expected if you love older men. You're finally left sitting alone on a bench.

"Companion, 47, seeks companion for mutual lashings with cane, switch, or whip. Please sign up here." I was aroused by the notice in the teahouse at the old train station, with wrought iron brackets and old lanterns, still standing from the time of the emperor. I scribbled an answer, giving the hour for an assignation and a sign by which we would spot each other.

A few days later I was parading up and down, pretending not to be interested, hands clasped behind my back—the signal—near the Ostkreuz train station. Then I saw him: young-looking despite his age, tall, slim, and wiry-athletic, a mixture of carefree street urchin and graceful cat. At the same time, he exuded that self-assurance which has always attracted me to certain men.

I was drawn to rough sex from early on. Even at school, I used to crane my neck when other students were thrashed with a cane, although I also felt sorry for them. As the thin stick whistled though the air, I'd hold my breath in a mingling of shame, mortification, and eroticism, and savor the thought of getting a few lashes on the behind myself. If the teacher grabbed me by the collar and I had to bend over, I knew that although the first lash would burn like fire, the second and third would not hurt but would instead arouse me.

The malicious, the philistines, and the moral apostles cry out when they don't understand something—and how little they understand— "That's disgusting, beyond our ken; it has to be sick, perverse, away with it." Let them keep psychologists busy with my sexual behavior; I don't torment myself with the question of how I got to be the way I am. It gives me pleasure, I don't hurt anyone with what I'm doing, to the contrary...so, what is wrong with it?

With beating heart, I rode with Jochen, my conquest from the train-station toilet, towards Mahlsdorf. Jochen loved to play games. I'll describe one: I brought my collection of short pants from the closet—corduroys, jeans, bathing trunks, leather pants—and spread them on the bed, while he wrote the numbers one to six on little slips of paper which he then assigned to the various pants. The next set of numbered slips was matched to various instruments of punishment: thin cane, thick cane, switch, whip, cat-o'-nine-tails. We then used a pair of dice to determine which pants went with the various switches. Then we multiplied the numbers by each other. The product determined the number of lashes I would give him or he would give me. In keeping with my personality, I always preferred the passive role. "My God, you handle the cane like a girl from an academy for young ladies," Jochen would tease me if I was not disciplinarian enough for him.

I was with him for twenty-seven years until his death in 1987. He was a gym teacher and had been a famous tennis player in the thirties. During the Third Reich, he had married a childhood friend, a lesbian, to be safe from the Nazis.

Jochen dominated me, and I liked being dominated. He advised me, made photos showing the progress of construction on the house, and reminded me to save all of the bills. I never would have thought of such a thing. To keep a household in order with a woman's touch is one thing, but with paperwork, I'm too careless; it's just not my style. Like a good wife, I did whatever Jochen told me. I admired what girls at the time looked for in men. They fascinated me if they made me feel protected, that I could count on them in time of need.

Chapter 16

THIS HOUSE IS MY FATE. It called out to me in its greatest need, and I was there for it. Here, my dream of having my own museum became reality. But more than that: this house is my home. Museum guide, tenant, and housekeeper all in one, I have furnished the house the way a middle-class housewife would have furnished her home around 1900. In this same late-baroque structure, I was examined by the school physician as a little tyke. The mansion has haunted me ever since. I was always checking to see how it was holding up as the years went by.

Built in 1780, it was first an official bureau for the township of Köpenick. In 1821, it was sold into private ownership. The wealthy Jewish merchant Lachmann bought it in 1869. He modernized it in the style of the time, adding folding doors with cornices and ornamental moldings over each doorway. He also had an exterior grand stairway with neoclassical stucco work built on the side facing the courtyard. The small terrace and the exterior steps on the park side were kept and merely restored. Throughout the house, Lachmann installed double windows with French partitions, those cross-shaped windows so popular at the time.

Lachmann's heirs sold the property. The last aristocratic landowners in "Mahlsdorf an der Ostbahn," as it was then known at the post office, were the Schrobsdorffs, a patrician family from Thüringen. The father of Renate Schrobsdorff, a niece of the poet Friedrich Rückert, preached for the Moravian Brethren in Rixdorf.

In 1920, the house came into the possession of the city of Berlin and was used as a children's home for ten years. When the local school moved in, the house was remodeled. Partitions were torn down to make space for four classrooms. It then alternately housed various offices: unemployment, identification, city hall, employment agency, then street cleaning, special classes, children's day care, juvenile bureau, finance, detective bureau, public library, school doctor's office, and kindergarten.

Since 1958, the house had been empty. One morning, as I was pitching along on the trolley car past the house, I saw a shutter hanging in the branches of a tree. I looked closer and got a terrible shock: the roof was full of holes, window panes broken, folding doors strewn about the garden.

I left the trolley and inspected the house from cellar to attic. In one year of standing empty, it had become a ruin. Vandals had torn out the floorboards and carried them off as kindling. They had removed the doorknobs. Toilet bowls and sinks in the upper rooms were smashed, as was the porcelain in the kitchen. Beautiful new oak cupboards lay demolished on the floor. They had dragged off everything that wasn't screwed or nailed down.

When I saw the destruction, I thought they had all gone mad. Not only had some philistines transformed this mansion so rich in history into a ruin, it was even more horrible that the bureaucracy had let them do it. *Who is in charge?* I asked myself. I went over to the neighboring estate and asked the steward, a nice man with a peasant's stolidity, what was to become of the house. "You mean the City Palace?" he asked. The people of Mahlsdorf called it the "City Palace" even though it was only a manor house. "A giant cottage with exterior stairway," Theodor Fontane called such structures. The steward, his head bent to one side, explained, "The thing will be torn down."

The last caretaker of the manor house was working as a ticket taker at the Mahlsdorf train station. That evening at half past nine, I went looking for him in his little house at the train crossing. Between departing and arriving trains, he told me that he had tried to save the house. He had boarded up the doors time after time, but they would always be broken down the next day.

I quickly resolved to move from the house where I was born in Mahlsdorf-Süd to the mansion. I had to save it from further destruction. I made up a place to sleep with a few blankets on the bare floor, and placing a shrill whistle next to me, I dozed off. I had put wooden beams with bricks piled on top against the doors that could not be bolted. That very night, someone tried to break into the house, and my "alarm construction" collapsed with a loud crash. Startled, I reared up, gave a shrill blow on the whistle and roared, "What's going on?" There was some brief knocking about and then silence. The uninvited guest had hurried away like the wind.

The Lichtenberg Bureau of Education was inflexible. Each time I presented my petition, I was informed that I could not obtain the house. A two hundred fifty thousand mark reconstruction cost had been rejected by the council. Instead, the politicians of the province had allotted money for its demolition in their budget: sixty thousand marks to pay for blowing up the stone foundation and the cellar vault. "As the money is allotted, so shall it be spent," was the socialist bureaucratic answer to my suggestion that the city could save sixty thousand marks if they accepted my offer.

This bit of Mahlsdorf history would have disappeared forever, had not accident—or rather socialist slovenliness—come to my aid.

The evicted kindergarten had found only temporary quarters in town, so the administration was searching for permanent quarters for the little boys and girls. They had their eye on the country house of a man in the moving business who had gone over to the West. As was then the custom, the administration confiscated the house.

In converting the house for use as a kindergarten, they had installed a coal-burning central heating system. But they had overlooked a crucial detail: a larger chimney.

The chimney sweep for the district shook his head. "I refuse to accept responsibility for this flue," he declared flatly, in his correct Prussian way, to the horrified woman in charge of the kindergarten, just before the official opening of the prestigious project. The cost of demolishing the old chimney from cellar to roof and constructing a new one was seventy thousand marks.

As I stood for the nth time in front of the door to the Department of Education, someone inside roared, "Where am I supposed to get seventy thousand marks for a new chimney? The demolition of the old shack in Mahlsdorf is already costing me sixty thousand."

Since the loud tirade went on and on, I just knocked and burst in. *The worst they can do is throw you out,* I decided. At that point, I just didn't care.

The face of the official in charge of domestic finances lit up as if a golden ass had materialized in front of him—which, if you think about it, I really was. Although his voice had shrilled in the highest register just before, he was now sweetness and amiability personified; rising from his desk, he greeted me in high spirits, "Here he comes! Do you still want that old shack?" Without waiting for an answer, he turned to the builder in charge of the kindergarten conversion and explained, "When this young man takes over the manor house in Mahlsdorf, sixty thousand marks will become available. We can get the rest of the money together somehow." Naturally, I was agreeable.

He gave the house over to me, however, without any written contract between us. I was only required to sign a paper stating that I undertook the work at my own risk. That way, the administration was assured of two things: on the one hand, they could throw me out whenever they wanted, and on the other, the city of Berlin assumed no responsibility if I fell while working on the roof. It didn't matter to me. I only wanted to save the house.

First, I had to put the place in order, a maddening task because every nook and cranny was packed with filth and broken glass. Little by little, I converted this ruin without heat, without water, without a toilet, and without windows into a house. I pulled hundreds of nails left behind by the previous tenants out of the remaining doors, window frames, and walls.

I wanted to resurrect the era between 1870 and 1900 by adhering to the merchant Lachmann's example; the house, modernized in the neoclassical style, harmonized beautifully with "my" Gründerzeit.

Even though the so-called "Gründerjahre" lasted only a short time—they began in 1871 after the Franco-German war and ended ingloriously with the depression of 1873, the "Gründerzeit crash"—the various fashions, furnishings and architecture of the years between 1870 and the turn of the century are considered to be in the Gründerzeit style.

Industrialization was proceeding rapidly. Machines turned products out more quickly, and because in greater quantity, more cheaply. Moldings and ogees could now be milled by machine; the decorative mountings stamped, pressed, or cast, whereas before each piece had to be done by hand.

An army of artists outdid themselves with ever-new designs. Furniture manufacturers copied, not always flawlessly, almost all the styles of the past, modifying them to suit the prevailing fashion. Single pieces as well as complete sets for salons, studies, living, dining, and bedroom furniture, and interiors for restaurants, apothecary shops, and bakeries were turned out in Romantic, Gothic, Renaissance, baroque, rococo, classical, and, after 1900, even in Empire and Biedermeier styles. These neo-styles are designated as Historismus. The most popular fashion—whether simply or elegantly finished—was the Neo-Renaissance style.

Even Art Nouveau, fashionable between 1900 and 1910, could not entirely supplant Historismus. Complete sets of furniture for rooms and kitchens were particularly in demand: silverware, chandeliers, stoves, doors, rugs. Everything had to be in proper style. The housings for technical instruments as well—music boxes, juke boxes, orchestrions, gramophones, telephones, sewing machines, and clocks—were made with loving attention to the details of the style in fashion.

But soon the wave of "functionalism" spilled over from America. Roll top desks, cupboards, and even the exterior of the Edison phonograph had to express their functions. Ornament was shunned. Around 1910, a reference book for the practical housewife advised, "A sideboard must not be sweet, or charming, nor a little church, or a robber baron's castle—it should not do anything but keep dust and flies off dinner plates and soup bowls." I am of another opinion. Scrolls and other ornamentation delight mankind. Everything today is so functional. True, coupon clipping and speculation scandals marked the Gründerzeit. The exceeding passion for expansion, the ostentation of factory owners and country squires, and the overweening pride of the Hohenzollern, "Under Germany's spell, the world is well," are mirrored, according to the critics, in the furniture. "The jumbled discord" is "unseemly and not quite human." Nonsense—for me, Gründerzeit furniture has form.

Although it was disparagingly named after Kaiser Wilhelm, Historismus has its origin in mid-century England, where the industrial revolution occurred earlier; the Victorian style came later. Historismus also caught on in France, Italy, Switzerland, Denmark, Poland, Russia, and Austria. Naturally, the columns of a dining-room sideboard in Paris looked different from the ones in Berlin, Vienna, Warsaw, or St. Petersburg.

I know Gründerzeit style is derivative, but nevertheless, I have an affinity for these things because they are charmingly proportioned. Professionals still turn up their noses at mention of Gründerzeit, in contrast to Art Nouveau, which followed Historismus and was despised as kitchy into the fifties, but after that, began its triumphant return.

Despite their raised eyebrows, art historians and museum curators have often come to see me over the years. I recall one of them quite clearly, his close-set eyes and his imbecilic question, "How in the world did you come to collect the Gründerzeit era?"

"I simply found and still find it beautiful. After all, the epoch of an earlier industrial age should be preserved for the future. Don't you see," I continued, sitting in the living room with him, "here, I have a feeling of security, of permanence. The bookcase with its columns, the wood-decorated sofa with matching chairs, table, and stools, the grandfather clock, the desk with its top, the piano with columns, the brass chandeliers, and the pieces with ornamental banisters—everything in Neo-Renaissance style; how carefully measured it all is—typical middle-class furniture from 1890—that's me!"

To that he could only reply, "Well, if you see it that way."

For me, it did not matter whether the furniture came from an upper-, middle- or working-class household. If I really think about it, I prefer middle-class pieces. I am too unpretentious to like showpieces; I would not want to be presented with a breakfront that has six doors and carved dwarfs—much too immodest and bombastic—but the pieces must not be too plain either.

I admire the Sanssouci Palace, the New Palais, the Sea Shell Hall, but I would not want to live there. The housewife in me would say, "Oh, so many windows to clean and so much dust to wipe away!" In those places, I would be divided into the noble lady and the housewife. When in doubt, the housewife would win out.

Before I could make my dream of having my own museum a reality, I had to shovel rubbish for three and a half years. The many partitions that had been installed later on the second floor were too heavy for the ceilings on the ground floor and they sagged almost eighteen centimeters in places. I tore these walls down and carted the rubble with horse and wagon to the dump. In 1962, a worker from the Bureau for the Preservation of Monuments looked around in amazement and asked, "Which company disposed of the rubble for you?" I raised both hands, "This is my company." I was told the house might be declared a historical monument. But nothing concrete happened. The Gründerzeit style was suspect, as was Lottchen.

Since the house no longer had doors or windows, mildew and wood-worms were everywhere. Mildew thrived because the second floor had been inappropriately used; bathrooms had been installed there for the children despite the paneled walls. The house was rotting. In order to work on the second floor safely, I built scaffolding and supported the ceilings in danger of collapsing with iron columns. I spent all year treating the rafters with wood preserver. A crazy drudgery, but I had fun anyway.

My know-how came from my work on the Friedrichsfelde Palace and from books. One of my friends, a statistician, took care of the calculations—mathematics has never been my forte.

On the practical side, I got a job as a night watchman at the estate next door. Mornings at six o'clock, I would throw my overalls into a corner, pull on my short leather pants, and without having touched my mattress, climb up on the roof. I sawed off the boards that were mildewed or worm-eaten. Then I carted new boards and roof tiles, with horse and wagon, from barns and stables in Biesdorf or Mahlsdorf. Once, I drove as far as the center of Berlin to buy and borrow old, seven-meter-long rafters on Ross Strasse. I got window frames from the VEB demolition depot where they were piled up around the courtyard.

"The nut is here again," the construction workers at condemned houses would greet me when I appeared. The Bureau for the Preservation of Monuments would let me know where buildings were being demolished in town. I could tell by their façades which houses were likely to have folding doors.

Thus I came to Prenzlauer Strasse and stopped in front of the baroque façade of the Mette Haus, named after the earlier owners, Adolf and Emilie Mette. A manor outside the gates in the outskirts of Spandau, it later sheltered an institution to train poor girls, often orphans, to be housekeepers.

I was ready to walk on, when a window on the ground floor opened and a crone, old as a piece of ivory, stuck her wizened head out, "You are looking at our beautiful old house with such interest. Too bad it will soon be torn down."

At my question about folding doors from the Gründerzeit, she and her sister invited me inside and proudly showed me the folding doors with moldings from around 1870. They had almost the same profile as the ones I still needed in Mahlsdorf.

Since the other apartments had already been vacated, the sisters, as last tenants, had the keys in their possession. I undertook, not only a very interesting tour of the house, but also decided to use one of the apartments as a storage place for the furniture I had collected in my expeditions through other condemned buildings.

I transported the three folding doors that I had removed from the Mette Haus to Mahlsdorf in a small truck owned by a carter named Philip. From neighboring houses I stripped door handles and frames, skirting boards, floorboards, stucco rosettes, bell ropes, banisters, and twenty-three door moldings.

One morning, on arriving at the Mette Haus, I found a large chunk of the baroque façade's plaster lying on the sidewalk. The iron cannon-ball fired by General Tettenborn in 1813 during the wars of liberation against Napoleon was still stuck in it. Someone had tried to extract it with a crowbar but had failed. I completed his task and brought the iron witness of a time gone by to the Märkische Museum where it can still be viewed today.

Although the basic structure was still flawless, the Registry Office building, constructed around the turn of the century by Ludwig Hoffmann on the Fischerinsel in the Fischerkiez section of Old Berlin, was to be torn down. I noticed, high under the gable, a Berlin Bear escutcheon made of sandstone and weighing many a hundredweight. I pressed twenty marks into the hand of the astounded man in charge of the blasting and begged him to blow up the gable in such a way that the escutcheon would be preserved. I watched the explosion from a safe distance. When the dust lifted, the stone, with the Berlin Bear undamaged, was lying on top of the heaped-up debris.

With another twenty, I enlisted the excavation foreman to transport the heavy sandstone relief. We tied it to the bulldozer with steel cables and drove at a walking pace to the Märkische Museum. Today, the stone still lies near the façade at the side entrance.

The workers thought me a little strange, but my passion for preserving everything also seemed to impress them. One confessed to me, "For the magistrate to destroy Fischerkiez, the cradle of Old Berlin, is a crime." Today, ugly concrete high-rise buildings tower where that section used to be. Only the Scheunenviertel retains an atmosphere of Old Berlin. In recent decades, the SED government deliberately permitted whole sections of the city, which had developed through time, to rot because they wanted to replace them with prefab houses by 1955 at the latest.

In those days, I often set out at night armed with hammer, pliers, crowbar, and screwdriver to remove stubborn door frames. Once, as I was roaming in the Scheunenviertel, up Wadzeck and Georgenkirchstrasse at three in the morning, I came upon a condemned building. With the help of a flashlight, I groped my way through the cellar and outbuilding.

Soon I spotted a door frame and went to work. I only became aware of all the noise I was making when I peeked through a broken window. Two policemen were approaching the house. "Just what are you doing here at this hour?"

"I'm dismantling a door frame."

The policeman directed the flashlight beam right on my face, came closer and called out, "Say, are you the guy with the museum who was written up in the newspaper a little while ago?"

"Yup, I'm the one."

At that, the policemen became helpful and brought me chairs—some from the thirties, of course, because they couldn't tell them from the ones made at the turn of the century—coffee grinders, and tubes for air valves.

After this collection, I went to the construction shack at the Mette Haus. "What brings you here so early in the morning?" the workman greeted me. I didn't have to wait long for them to get the tractor going and drive back to the Scheunenviertel. The policeman had been standing guard with this dog. "Nothing stolen," he grinned. We loaded everything up and brought it to my place.

The day was drawing near when the Hirschfeld sisters had to move to their tight new quarters in Friedrichshagen. We took sad leave of each other. Although their new apartment had modern facilities, both women always longed for their old domicile on Prenzlauer Strasse.

The construction workers and I got along very well. If I pressed a twenty or a fifty into their hands, they became enthusiastic. "Sure we'll pull a beam out for you. If you need more doors, take these, and pull off those stucco rosettes." I remember at one house I was still fiddling around with the rosettes while the workers were drilling holes for explosives. The one with the big loudspeaker horn happened to look up from the courtyard. When he saw me still laboring away at the ceiling, he hollered up in the broadest Berlin dialect, "Hey, you, screw off your rosettes and get out or we'll blow you up wit'em!"

He meant it as a joke, but that scene symbolized what was going on. I could almost never save as much as was being destroyed. If I received notice from the Bureau for the Protection of Monuments about a condemned building, all too often by the time I got there only a field of debris was left. When it came to the destruction of entire sections of the city, socialism proceeded with capitalist efficiency and speed. At least I was able to snatch a few condemned things from the blasting and wrecking crews of the Berlin sixties and seventies.

I am not concerned with dead stones or lifeless furniture. They are embodiments that mirror the history of the men who built them, who lived in them. Senseless destruction does away with a former way of life, the foundation of our spiritual and aesthetic culture, and irretrievably impoverishes our daily lives.

My driving need has always been to preserve things, not for myself, but for posterity, to establish a continuity, not a senseless ending. I am inspired by that idea. *Whatever you can accomplish with your two hands,* I thought, *you must do.* Often I wished for more hands to save, for example, Schloss Schöneiche or Schloss Fredersdorf, demolished as recently as the eighties.

I dismantled everything so carefully that nothing ever broke. I preserved every screw that attached a doorbell. Salvaged banisters were numbered and kept in my museum until I needed them. Visitors to the exhibition think that the door handles, the molding, the carved door trim and ledges have always been here. Not so. But I am naturally a bit proud that everything fits together well enough to give that impression.

I questioned housewives, old ladies, and servants employed in those days to learn what pieces stood in a Gründerzeit living or dining room and how they had been arranged. I pored over furniture catalogues from the days of the Empire that I had found in junk shops during the war. I rummaged through antique shops and got lucky: *The Practical Housewife* from the year 1900, or *I Can Run a Household* from 1890. They usually contained advice about etiquette, running a household, and furnishing an apartment. Strangely enough, I found everything so right, as if made for me, that I became a perfect housewife of the Gründerzeit.

The first guided tour through Mahlsdorf on August 1, 1960 happened by accident. Workmen repairing the trolley rails, gardeners from the park, and people working on the neighboring farm had started saying to each other, "Hey, we got to go in there and see what's going on." After work, they appeared, along with some curious passers-by who had joined them. I had finished furnishing two rooms: a living room of the 1890 era, still the second stop in my tours, and a dining room, which I removed the following year to make space for the Neo-Gothic room.

Word about my museum spread. In the local pubs, the farmers and townsmen of Mahlsdorf were telling each other, "There's a big automatic music machine with sheet-metal records he plays for you." Even though the walls had not been renovated and straw was still hanging from the ceilings, people were enthusiastic and found it interesting. Brigades of workmen, school children, art students and, naturally, colleagues from other museums visited me.

Chapter 17

SINCE 1963, THE CENTERPIECE of my collection, the "driest pub" in Berlin, has been set up in the cellar of the Mahlsdorf mansion. I had driven to Mulackstrasse in the Scheunenviertel to get some furniture from the "Mulackritze." As I made my way through the narrow streets, I did not suspect that I had been called to one of the most famous pubs of Old Berlin. Despite the seedy house fronts, the tiny shops, the peeling plaster, it all seemed a pleasing contrast to the monstrosities of nearby Alexanderplatz.

In the Scheunenviertel, you could get one on the kisser faster than anywhere in Berlin. Dives, saloons, and junk shops, whores, shysters, dawdlers, and petty thieves have made up the scene since the turn of the century. At one time, the barns of Berlin farmers were located there, hence the name: the quarter of barns. An elector's decision that barns belonged outside the city gates resulted in the Scheunenfeld, an area of lanes with twenty-seven barns. At the end of the eighteenth century, the barns had to make way for domestic dwellings, cramped crooked houses set into narrow streets.

As in no other section of the city, the rulers at the time tried to impose their stamp on this ancient part of Berlin—but in vain. So utterly had the tight streets, the tiny courtyards, the miserable apartments, and the cellar dungeons gone to the dogs, even by the time of Kaiser Wilhelm II, that he wanted to have the entire quarter razed to the ground. Life raged at its most basic level in the crowded maze of streets. Whores and their "protectors" slipped in and out of the taverns—almost all unlicensed—taking their broth together with respectable citizens and workers of the neighborhood.

After the First World War, someone else raged there: the social democratic "bloodhound" Gustav Noske who delivered the inhabitants of the entire quarter to the firing squad after the Spartacus Insurrection. Colonel Reinhard, commanding officer of the Berlin troops, justly nicknamed "The Butcher of Berlin," carried out the offensive for the retaking of the streets around Alexanderplatz. Noske's order, "Anyone caught fighting with weapon-in-hand against government troops is to be shot at once," was broadened by the vigorous colonel to read, "Furthermore, all inhabitants of houses from which our troops are fired on, whether they protest their innocence or not, are to be brought out into the street and the house is to be searched for weapons in their absence. Suspicious characters in whose homes weapons are found are to be shot." In the narrow alleys of the Scheunenviertel, the proven measures from the battlefields of the First World War were put into action, from flamethrowers on top of tanks to heavy howitzers. One can imagine what that meant in the overpopulated quarter. Even today, it is best to draw the curtain on the scenes that took place in the streets around Alexanderplatz because of that insane order given in March of 1919.

But the Scheunenviertel survived, and the effort of the Weimar Republic to bring fresh air and light to the quarter—the reason for its destruction—was left half-done.

Next, Polish Jews came to the Scheunenviertel. Life, which took place almost entirely in the streets, changed. Figures from the demimonde and underworld were now joined by harried Jewish merchants with long curled sidelocks, covered heads, and striking caftans, who roamed the crowd, here and there, praising the garments on their arms.

By the twenties, next to the slogans for Liebknecht and Luxemburg, "Heil Hitler" was scrawled on the walls with greater frequency. After the "take-over," the brownshirts memorialized their martyr, their company commander and pimp, Horst Wessel, with a Horst Wessel House, a Horst Wessel Street, and a Horst Wessel Theater.

On the evening of January 14, 1930, a widow, at whose home Wessel resided, registered a complaint against her tenant at the local Communist Party headquarters. The whore who worked for him was living at his place, but he refused to pay the additional rent. The men on duty, with "Ali" Höhler from Mulackstrasse at the head, set out to give the brownshirt lay poet a good beating. It came to a scuffle during which Höhler, pimp and member of the sport league Evertrue, shot Wessel. When Wessel died of his injuries a month later, the Gauleiter of Berlin, Joseph Goebbels, declared the twenty-three-year-old a savior. His song, *"Raise high the flag, our ranks in tight formation...,"* became the second German national anthem in the Third Reich. Ali Höhler, condemned to six years for his deed, was delivered over to the SA and brutally murdered by the brownshirts.

"15 TAVERN 15" was written in large plaster letters across the front of Mulackstrasse 15 when I paid my first visit to the tavern in 1960. The last mistress of the pub came shuffling towards me. The hair that had been untamed, black, almost African, was now gray, thin, and lifeless. She peered at me through thick eyeglasses, and greeted me: Minna Mahlich, afflicted and marred by fate. If her dark, clear eyes had not been undisguisedly curious and sparkling with life, I would have taken her for a bag lady.

I bought a standing clock, table and chairs, a sideboard, and a buffet. The history of the house interested me, and Minna Mahlich obliged. Built in 1770, it had been an inn until 1952. In the twenties, Sodkes Schankwirtschaft, its official name, served many illustrious guests. In 1920, Henry Porten shot a movie there called *The Girl from Ackerstrasse*, filled with the local color of the Old Berlin Scheunenviertel. In 1929, the upstairs rooms were used in *Mother Krausen's Trip to Fortune*, a film about the fate of a poor Berlin proletarian family immediately after the First World War.

Artists, actors, and literati came here to drink their beer because the Mulackritze was a so-called "wild place." Among the thieves, prostitutes, and gays for sale moved the most talked about celebrities in bohemian Berlin: Fritzi Massary, the grand lady of Berlin theater; Claire Waldoff; Max Pallenberg; Bertold Brecht, who was also a guest there after the war; Hubert von Meyerinck; Gustaf Gründgens; Paul Wegener; Wilhelm Bendow; Siegfried Breuer; and the heavenly Dietrich, then still a chubby, unknown actress.

Isa Vermehren, a famous singer in the twenties, was also a frequent visitor. Imprisoned by the Nazis for being a lesbian, she was deported to the women's KZ, Ravensbrück. Fortunately, she was freed in 1945 and performed again at the tavern, singing her couplets in a boyish voice, accompanied by an accordion. She is still alive today, having relinquished her hectic surroundings for a secluded convent.

Heinrich Zille fashioned his genre paintings in the Mulackritze while his little daughter was being rocked on the lap of a whore or pimp. Decades later, Margarete Köhler-Zille visited the Mulackritze again, this time located in the cellar of my Gründerzeit Museum. Aged but hale, she stood at the bar, her hand stroking the metal counter top. With shining eyes, she told me how on hot days, while her father was drawing at his table in the corner, she had cooled her nose on the edge of the metal.

Even in the time of the Empire, the Jewish sex researcher Magnus Hirschfeld spent time at the Mulackritze. By then, the tavern had already become an El Dorado for gays, lesbians, and transvestites. Occasionally, the Tuesday Society for women in men's clothing and the Thursday Society for men in women's attire, as well as the sport and benevolent societies, Immertreu and Felsenfest, met there. Up to eight whores solicited for the shop and had their "work rooms" in the attic.

Chairs and beer mugs flew through the bar during rough-and-tumble fights. "Traveling Arthur," particularly brutal, with hands like toilet seat covers, shot the very young Ida Krüger because she did not want to share her earnings as a barmaid and drinking companion with him. Thanks to a thick corsage, she survived.

The sport and benevolent society, Immertreu, changed taverns in the twenties, moving from the Mulackritze to a dive on Breslauer Strasse 1. One evening, they had gathered there in top hats and tails to drink to the burial of a member of their group. At the time, a subway was being built under the Frankfurter Allée. And so it happened that after work, laborers from the subway construction came to the same dive where the sport society folk were gathered. The members of the Immertreu, while not particularly sensitive about dishing it out, were very sensitive when their honor was challenged.

When a particularly rowdy construction worker pummeled the collapsible top hat of a worthy mourner, then placed the battered object on his own head, a veritable free-for-all ensued. All the furniture in the saloon was broken—the piano player moved the piano away from the wall and crouched behind it to protect himself from the glasses, bottles, chairs, table legs, and later, entire tables being hurled in every direction. The turmoil had moved into the street by the time the "men in blue" arrived, closed off Breslauer Strasse and dove into the fracas. No one could tell friend from foe as the locals from nearby houses took advantage of the occasion to get their licks in. The whores soon joined the fun, throwing flowerpots from their little upper-story love chambers to ensure that the merry turmoil would not slow down. When the ladies ran out of flowerpots, they hit on a spicier idea: emptying their overflowing chamber pots on the combatants. Even in the sixties, people were still talking about that street fight as the most imposing one Berlin had ever seen.

All in all, violent crimes remained the exception. As a rule, anyone who misbehaved was put over a table in the bar, his bottom bared, while everybody had fun giving him a whack.

Up in the garret, "love and lash" were practiced on demand: S/M sex, with whip or cane, on a suitable stand. There, to modify the familiar words of Frederick the Great, everyone could reach bliss according to his sexual taste. This freedom intrigued the brave explorer, Magnus Hirschfeld, who with his kindly eyes and drooping mustache looked like a helpful grandfather. The scene at the Mulackritze offered him plenty of material for his enlightening books.

Although I never met him in person, I owe a great deal to Magnus Hirschfeld. His books reassured me that, as a transvestite, I was not alone in the world. Hirschfeld coined the perhaps false but at least epoch-defining term "the third sex" to describe homosexuals. As a specialist in sexual pathology and an expert witness at many trials, he had made it his duty to prove through research that people must not be condemned and thrown into jail for what is looked upon by most of society as "perverse and unnatural," that such behavior was not criminal, but diseased, or perhaps only "different." His life's work, no matter what one thinks of his theses today, was filled with a spirit of great humanitarianism, because in addition to his desire for knowledge, his work was based on a deep sympathy for all that is human. That the Nazis thought him an "old swine" is not surprising. One May evening in 1933, at the bonfire of books in Berlin, they burned not only his books but a doll with Hirschfeld's features. Goebbels and his henchmen left no doubt as to what would have happened to Hirschfeld had he not been on a world tour when the Nazi brutality began. Thus, he was able to lounge on the shores of the Mediterranean for two years until the natural end of his life in 1935.

Under Fritz Brandt, who owned the Mulackritze from 1921 to 1945, the pub had remained a place for gays, lesbians, and transvestites to hang out. If people whom no one knew and who were suspected of being informers came in, Brandt would put a Nazi record on the gramophone so that everyone was warned and didn't blab anything incriminating.

Without much education, Brandt, an innately kind man, also had pluck and courage. Since he was married, he could have thrown out the "undesirables" and made the Mulackritze into a "respectable" place. But no, opportunism was not his thing. His heart belonged to the whores, the gays, the lesbians, and the transvestites. Although people did stick together in the quarter, Brandt went further than that: he helped the last few transvestites who had to go underground to survive by feeding them throughout the war. No longer registered with the police, they could not apply for food ration cards, and so, their Mulackritze host served them their usual order, mostly turnip stew—which only cost five groschen during the war—in the back room. After the tavern closed for the night, this insignificant hero, to whom no one has dedicated a memorial, would let the transvestites earn a little money by helping in the kitchen or cleaning up. That way, they not only stayed alive, but also preserved their dignity.

Since the brownshirts thought of them as "human scum," Fritz Brandt was risking his life with his "degenerate" behavior of hiding the transvestites from their clutches. It was not easy to keep his act secret since, during the last years of the war in particular, the SS would stage raids in the Scheunenviertel. Even the ruins and destroyed air-raid shelters were gone over with dogs while searching for so-called "enemies of the Wehrkraft" and deserters.

Since Mulackstrasse 15 only had one room and a storage place without doors in its cellar for beer, you could only get into the tavern from the front entrance. It was thus useful to keep an eye on the street. In the event of a trap, Fritz Brandt had planned ahead and engaged someone as a look-out. If the SS approached, the look-out would blow a shrill whistle. At that, the transvestites would hitch up their skirts, step on the dustbin, slip over the wall, climb up the roof of the shed, and from there, it was only a short leap to a stable and then on to the Garnisons Cemetery. There, these women in the bodies of men, who would never consent to carrying a weapon, could hide in the mausoleum. That way, many who without the brave tavern keeper would have been smoke in the wind of Auschwitz survived: beautiful Vera, as fragile as a flower of glass, or Ruth, with her brown, shiny hair, cherry-colored lips, and dark-sherry eyes.

"Is there anything still left of the tavern?" I asked Minna Mahlich. Old tavern furnishings, with the odor of thousands of cigarettes mixed with the smell of roasts and beer fumes, have always fascinated me. All of that, along with the music blaring from the gramophone, creates the atmosphere of a tavern.

"Sure you can see the pub. It's still here." She got out the key and an old enameled flashlight since the place didn't have electric lights. Spider webs hung from the ceiling to the counter of the bar. Stacks of briquettes were heaped in front. The tavern had in the meantime been degraded to a coal cellar. A block for chopping wood stood in the center, with pieces of wood lying around it. But the old bottles and glasses were neatly arranged in the rack behind the counter, the gramophone still stood on the bar, and the regulator clock hung on the wall.

The "Dancing Forbidden" sign, which Fritz Brandt had nailed up to save the music charge, hung there along with the sign forbidding whores, "Prostituted are forbidden to enter these premises." Brandt had not quite conquered the art of orthography. Below it was the postscript, somewhat of a joke, "according to police regulations." That way, the girls knew that he had nothing against it. Another sign prohibited "Klammern," really "Klaverjas," a Jewish card game.

Next to the gramophone with the funnel speaker stood the old hunger tower, the display case that stored cures for a rumbling stomach: pickled eggs, pickled herring, and so forth. A gingerbread heart made of plaster of Paris, an advertisement, meant that the tavern was fully licensed—the guests could even stuff themselves with cake. I regarded the pictures and beer ads hung everywhere, and said jubilantly, "The whole thing is perfect Neo-Renaissance, about 1890!"

"You got it. 1890—that's when the furniture was made." With wit and humor, this authentic Berlin tavern keeper had, despite the Nazis and the SED members, preserved her cheeky insolence. Minna Mahlich's maiden name was Levinthal. She survived the Nazi Reich only because her husband, Alfred, an "Aryan," remained loyal to her.

The National Socialist authorities, the Gestapo, and the police, had constantly bothered him, "Get divorced from the old stinking Jew and marry an Aryan girl," they snarled at him. But he had the nerve to say, "You know, you've got to let me handle that. I swore to be faithful to my wife at the altar, and I'm gonna keep my vows." A truly Christian-minded man with spunk.

Before the war, the Mahlichs both waited on customers in the Mulackritze. After the so-called "Reichskristallnacht" in 1938, Minna Mahlich was prohibited from working on the premises. She was lucky that her husband survived the war. If he had been killed in battle, she would have been deported to KZ at once. Fritz Brandt died shortly after the war. Minna Mahlich took care of him as well as she could to the very end. During the war, she was assigned to forced labor. She had to drag bags of cement, coal, and heavy sacks of potatoes at the Lehrter freight station. Summer and winter, day and night. It was particularly base and vile that the Jewish women were not allowed to wear coats while working, not even in the worst cold.

But Minna Mahlich stuck it out, and in 1945, she and her husband took over the tavern. It didn't take long for the old guests to come back: film, radio, and theater people, gays, lesbians, transvestites, and whores. Once again, there was dancing to the gramophone and pianola. But the silence of the capricious authorities was deceptive and short-lived. Even before the establishment of the Deutschen Demokratischen Republik, or DDR, there were problems. One day, as the usual customers were gathered in the bar, an official from town hall appeared and declared in a raucous voice, "Mrs. Mahlich, if you don't throw out the prostitutes, lesbians, and gays, we'll take away your liquor license and close up shop." Minna Mahlich, from her place behind the bar, blew up. "You've got nerve to say that to me, a victim of National Socialism! I thought those days were over and done with."

Those days may have been over, but the new lords had their own notion of manners and morality. They took away her "victim of fascism" pension of over four hundred marks a month, and on February 26, 1946, they took away her liquor license. Only after she submitted a formal complaint, and after the Russians assumed command, was the order to close rescinded. But the borough officials were not pleased, and obviously went to work on the Russian commander. A new missive from town hall, dated March 23, 1946, came fluttering into the Mulackritze. With barely restrained triumph, it announced that the Russian command had in the meantime confirmed the order to close. This decree was later rescinded only by accident. The East Berlin Anti-Fascist Resistance Committee had invited Minna Mahlich's brother, Dr. Max Levinthal from Brussels, co-founder of the resistance there, to a meeting. When he intervened with the magistrate on his sister's behalf, the bureaucrats there were made painfully aware that their anti-fascist reputation could be damaged. Minna Mahlich's liquor license was re-issued; however, her pension was reinstituted only from the date the decision to rescind became official, and not retroactively, as would have been fair. They also peevishly did not neglect to demand an administrative fee of one hundred Reichsmarks for renewal of the liquor license.

For a few years, she was left in peace, but that respite was followed by a lesson straight out of the Stalinistic, bureaucratic horror cabinet. The local police was prodded into acting against the bar, and soon the verdict was out: "Since, as a result of a recent police inquiry, you have been found to be lacking in the soundness of character necessary for the operation of a public house...." The message, in a letter dated October 10, 1951, claimed that it was necessary to rescind her permit to pursue the trade, effective at once. Sarcastically, the notice concluded that because the permit to operate a public house had been withdrawn by the police chief himself, there could be no further recourse to a legal remedy.

What it meant by lacking in "soundness of character" was obvious: to allow whores, gays, and lesbians in a bar was, according to the SED government, so blatantly unsocialist and indecent that there must be immediate intervention. Any delay would be dangerous. Thirty-one other taverns in the Spandauer outskirts were shut down following the closing of the Mulackritze. Practically overnight, the tavern life of the Scheunenviertel was done away with.

The magistrate had cleaned out the quarter and was satisfied. Only Mulackstrasse 15 was granted a ten-year grace period.

Less grace was extended in the second act. A brief notification of October 24, 1961 read: "For the realization of propositions connected with the rebuilding of Berlin, your property, located in the rebuilding zone of Berlin, will be requisitioned." "Rebuilding," in the language of the socialists who wanted to level everything, meant the disfiguring of the Scheunenviertel with look-alike, dull buildings. Naturally, the corresponding paragraphs, which declared the decree for such expropriation legally valid, were in good order. The Department of Finance for the District Office laid claim to the house and apprised the Mahlichs of the amount due to them in accordance with the Berlin "law of compensation" of April 25, 1960: seven thousand, seven hundred marks for a house that was almost two hundred years old and whose structure was in perfect order.

The curtain to the third act rose with the next notice that advised the Mahlichs to open an account at the Savings Bank of the City of Berlin so that the compensation could be remitted to them. Minna and Alfred Mahlich were not allowed to dispose of the entire pitiful sum at will; they were only permitted to withdraw the money in dribbling installments.

In December 1963, the final curtain fell on the tavern so full of Berlin history and local color: the house was torn down. Today, in 1992, only an iron railing, the length of the little house, stands in its place.

Back in 1960, when I stood in the pub for the first time and raved about the wonderful bar, Minna regarded me with her wise eyes and asked my name. I answered, "Berfelde."

"No, you chatterbox," she laughed cheerfully, "I want to know your first name." She looked at me slyly, "So, Lothar, you were also born on the seventeenth of May," a reference to the then still valid Homosexual Paragraphs 175. It was so unexpected that my face changed color, but she laughed, "You don't have to get so red, believe me, you gays were always my favorite guests, never made no trouble."

Male prostitutes were also welcome guests in the Mulackritze. Coming from Stein or Linienstrasse where they plied their trade, they warmed themselves among whores and "normal" guests. Sometimes, they brought their suitors along and let them buy drinks.

High above the tavern was the gable room, called the soldiers' room in the eighteenth century, and later, the visitors' or servant quarters. During my tour of the house, as I ascended the narrow stairs and entered the gable room, I noticed the simple windows with wrought iron catches. *That's nice,* I thought. The old muslin curtains were dusty and threadbare; dead flies were scattered on the windowsill—nobody had cleaned here in years.

Two beds were placed to the left and right of the window; under it stood a small table. To the left of the door, there was a small stove with a chaise lounge next to it. As was her custom, Minna Mahlich minced no words in explaining the most recent function of the picturesque little room, "This was the whores' room. Always busy. A short business discussion down below, a quick dash up for half an hour, some could do it in ten minutes. Both beds were taken, usually at the same time. Even the chaise. Just imagine, that screen there in the corner opened up, and they couldn't see each other. But from the chaise lounge, you could see both of them," Minna Mahlich explained. I blushed to my ears.

Since I wanted to keep everything from the tavern together, I inspected the entire house to the last corner. In one of the upper side rooms, with small doors next to the beds, I noticed some locked chests and an old wooden stand. "That's the whipping post. This is where S/M was done. The whips are in the black chest; get 'em out."

"I would very much like to take the chest with me," I said shyly.

She looked at me. "Be honest, you want what's in it too. Take 'em all, the whipping post too. Has anyone ever given it to you with a whip like this?" she asked, and without waiting for an answer, she took out a long, firm dog whip.

"Yes, yes, I've had it," I stammered.

"Well then, lay down over the post." Minna Mahlich measured the distance for a moment, and the whip whistled through the air and cracked against my short leather pants as if a shot had been fired. "See, everything can still be used," she laughed.

I had stumbled into a gay bar where everything suited my mentality. There, S/M could be practiced between women and women, men and men, and naturally, by the whores who let their behinds be thrashed, or took the active part with submissive lovers.

While Minna and I were loading the furniture, an elegant lady wearing a long, tight-waisted coat and extravagant hat walked by on the other side of the street. She was leading three Pekinese dogs, who seemed like intermingled balls of wool, on three red leashes. All at once, Minna hollered across the street, "Hey, Vera, you scum! Don't you know anybody anymore?" The lady turned around and the dogs rolled pell-mell across the street.

"Ah, too bad that everything has to go," fluted the delicate person.

"It's all going to Mahlsdorf," Minna said, pointing at me, "he's got a museum."

"Oh, one of these days I'll visit it then." The lady disappeared, and I was somewhat puzzled: the elegant coat, the beautiful earrings, and the little dogs—had she been in business in this area as a whore for the tavern?

"The lady is a guy," Minna said dryly when she saw my puzzled expression. "Beautiful Vera used to work for our place," she continued, "ever since she was fifteen years old. Little Vera always had paying suitors, never drank her money away, and her jewelry—don't fool yourself—is real. She was a male royal whore."

Up through the sixties and seventies, the SED government was eager to get rid of gays. And so, there was Vera with her Pekinese at the border crossing of Friedrichstrasse, ready to move into the new world of West Berlin. The entire circle of her friends and acquaintances had formed a lane in the customs office. They broke out in an ovation, beating pot covers together while some serenaded her by playing through their combs, *"Must I then, must I then, leave my own little town...."*

Vera handed a customs official her papers. But he wouldn't let her pass. "You are a woman, but there is a man's name given on your identification card. If you are a man wearing women's clothing, we can't let you through."

At that, Vera darlinged, "Even if you have never come across such an experience, sweetheart, you have to get used to it."

The customs official, completely put out, went to summon an officer. He soon appeared, accompanied by men leading a bunch of German shepherds. They ordered the taunting crowd of gays to leave the premises, probably out of fear that they would overturn the barriers. Finally giving up, the officials sheepishly let Vera through.

When I was allowed to travel "abroad" into the western part of the city, I wanted to see her again, but it was too late. Her death was as spectacular, grotesque, gruesome, and yet somehow ordinary, as were most of the episodes of her life. Wearing a dress and apron, having just cleaned her house, a dustbin still in her hand, Vera fell down the steps and broke her neck. Until the very end, she ran around the neighborhood in a dress. As a woman she had lived, and as a woman she was buried. Many followed her coffin, almost as many as were at the burial of Elli from the Beerhall.

But back to Minna Mahlich, that Berlin original. If the doorbell rang unmercifully, at least fifteen times, or if, in addition, anyone beat against the entrance with a cane, I always knew who would be standing there: Minna. "Lottchen, open up, the Mahlich woman is here."

Sometimes she would participate in the Sunday tours along with twenty-five others, and when we reached the last stop, the Mulackritze, she would stand there panting, slide her finger across the metal top of the bar and whinny, "Lottchen, you slut, you haven't polished the top again."

"Ladies and gentlemen, a historic moment. Here is the last hostess of the Mulackritze, Minna Mahlich," I would call out to the astounded visitors, and they would all applaud.

On April 5, 1971, a few years before her death, Minna made her final appearance at the Mulackritze. It was her seventieth birthday, and

I had invited the press. A team from the Berlin radio station had also come to interview her.

While the tape innocently turned, the radio people began to feel more and more indisposed, their faces turning from a spotty violet to ash-gray. They had not expected Minna Mahlich, roundly dominating the scene from behind her old place at the bar, to tell the stories of her surroundings just as riotously and unvarnished as they had occurred. Among the stories she told was the one about the beautiful young blonde whose lover had hoisted up her skirt in the private room of the Mulackritze. Minna had been on her way to the kitchen at the time, and had peeked at the blonde and her customer sitting on a bench. "And what could be seen?" Minna Mahlich asked the unhappy group of silent journalists. She raised both index fingers twenty centimeters apart and burst out laughing, "His tail between his garter straps!"

The radio people looked at each other in dismay. Obviously, such a sentence could not be transmitted in their socialist society. When her contribution was sent over the air, Minna Mahlich's deft, true-to-life stories were so neatly spliced for propriety, that even a pastor's daughter could take pleasure in them. Oh, how rigidly proper everyone was during socialism—here, even sex was practiced in the "old German" way.

Chapter 18

MUSEUM, FURNITURE, MEN. In 1963, I was called to inspect a standing clock with columns at Rosa-Luxemburg Strasse. As I came up on Alexanderplatz, I met him: very handsome, tall, thick hair, long summer pants, his jacket loosely flung over his arm—a virile Adonis. It was hard to tell his age. Although he gave an impression of youth and resiliency, he exuded at the same time an air of calm and composure that inspired trust, the kind of feeling that only good-natured people who have grown gray with honor possess. He gave me one glance that went through my entire being. I was wearing my short black leather pants, wooden clogs, and carrying a purse. I had lightheartedly come out of the underground, and on seeing him, my heart stood still. A spark passed between us. I turned my head after him; he did the same and beckoned to me. I was torn. Should I forget about the clock? For a moment, the yes's and no's were waging a war inside me, but the victory went—to the clock.

I was terribly disappointed when the standing clock with columns supposedly made of walnut in the year 1890 turned out to be Flemish, à la Danzig baroque from 1910. I no longer think about the clock, but I certainly remember that man. There are moments in life that haunt you years later because you think you have missed out on something. Whether you have really missed out on something wonderful is hard to tell, but you imagine you have.

At about the same time, I got to know Tutti, whose name was really Peter. She took care of the animals on the farm next to the museum. Six thousand pigs wallowed in the sty. Some of them I had farrowed myself, even though I was employed there only as a watchman. When I see work to be done, I do it. That's my nature. I don't like to sit around. And besides, simple people only care how hard you work. At a certain point, nobody at the farm paid any attention if they saw me wearing a woman's apron and a kerchief.

Men whose delicate bodies are in sharp contrast with their acquiline profiles and the determination expressed in the cleft of their chins have always attracted my attention. Red-blond, tiny Tutti seemed much too delicate for the heavy labor of taking care of those animals. I suspected that we were similarly disposed. Dressed as girls—she in a gray-green dress, I in blue—blond wigs rummaged out of the cupboard, eyebrows penciled in, and pumps slipped on, Tutti and I pranced to the station and rode to Berlin center.

"Hey cuties," the farm workers whom we met on the way greeted us, not recognizing us in our masquerade, even though they saw us every day. "Mom and daughter are out to have fun," the workers shouted after us. Tutti, being much smaller, was convinced that only she could have been taken for the "daughter" and gave me a triumphant look. The other people on the train seemed puzzled, and after examining us carefully, grumbled, "They're probably women," the usual reaction to my being neither one or the other.

If I went shopping wearing my wine-red ladies' coat, kerchief, and ladies' shoes, the salesladies looked at me cross-eyed, put their heads together, and whispered to each other. Then one would waddle to the back and quack, "Hey, come up front, Luzi in the red coat is here again to get her cheese and buttermilk."

I didn't hold it against them because they meant no harm. It was only curiosity. I would politely say good-bye, and after a short time, I stopped being a side-show for them. Today, most salespeople don't notice that I'm not the older woman they take me for. Others are not so sure. But they serve me. On the other hand, if I appeared in men's clothing, it sometimes happened that the salesladies split their sides laughing. I could never tell what put them in such high spirits. My shopping basket? My soft voice? My feminine movements? They instinctively had the right reaction. Masculine outfits just aren't right for me. They make me feel ill at ease. When I wear a dress or a ladies' coat, it feels right. People have a way of noticing when one is at ease with oneself.

But back to Tutti and our parties and excursions. She occupied a six-room suite in a meandering red brick building from the early 1900s called The Red Ox. Out of the huge number of households being dissolved, I had procured bedroom, dining room, study, parlor and ballroom furniture for Tutti, which she arranged with feminine good taste.

In Tutti's wooden-floored ballroom, furnished with the lower half of a huge Flemish buffet, with two gramophones from the twenties supplying the atmosphere, many DDR transvestites could, for the first time, act out their otherness. What rowdy times we had there!

Here a colorful, spicy mixture of life gathered—the spice found mainly among the lesbians. An owner of a dog salon from Köpenick, wearing a man's suit and a fake beard, appeared with her friend who favored another beard-wearing creature and was for that reason soundly beaten by her determined friend. Tutti wanted to intervene. "Another word, and you'll get a doozy from me," warned the poodle dresser, hands on hips, and pumping herself up like a trunkfish. My one thought was *Danger!* On the other hand, Tutti, not blessed with my woman's intuition, had a big mouth. She took a hit on the chest and tumbled behind the sofa. With her legs up in the air, her gray-green dress, as well as her slip, slid up. "Boy, Tutti, have you got thin thighs," taunted a lesbian, as the women's squabble moved to the verandah. Everybody laughed, and in a short time—men fight, women reunite—the dog-salon lady and her friend were again sitting together, blissfully smiling.

I later performed a small part with the pugnacious one in the DEFA film *Fleur Lafontaine.* Wearing her false beard, she played the bully, stomping through the twenties scene, while I was a fragile beauty in a black taffeta dress.

Ah, the silver screen! My first contact with it was in 1942. "Theater and Film Rental, Willy Porte" read the sign at 24 Lange Strasse as I, invited by the very same Mr. Porte, paid a visit to his prop storehouse. His place positively reeked of the world of film. Whole storehouse floors filled with Biedermeier rooms: salons, studies, and bedrooms; frying pans and bedpans, nothing was missing. Only the backdrop was built in the studio. Porte supplied the desired interior. Complete settings, from bakery to bar, waited here to be inserted in a Ufa film.

Porte needed phonograph cylinders for the next production. It was the first time I received an honorarium for lending them.

Years later, I happened to be walking through Tempelhof one day in 1959 and saw Willy Porte's familiar sign on a barn in Old Tempelhof. I peered through the windows of the stable that served as a storehouse. "Hey, don't we know each other?" asked Porte who, white-haired and heavy, was sitting on a chair in the small office and was examining me with his blank button-eyes in a friendly way. On the spot, I repaired an automated music player for him that was desperately needed and no longer made a sound. He paid me in Western currency, of enormous value for someone from the East.

Beginning with the sixties, prop men from Babelsberg and Adlerhof started turning up at the museum to ask for gramophones, records, and gas lamps. The directors knew how to value my expertise. When movies taking place in Gründerzeit days were being filmed, I was hired as an adviser. I shipped Gründerzeit furniture to Babelsberg if the DEFA storeroom couldn't come up with anything. I supplied the directors with authentic furniture for their sets. In the mid-sixties, the director of a new film project visited me and decided, beaming at me, "You've got a complete tavern. Why drag it to Babelsberg? We'll film here."

The man in charge of settings invited me to Babelsberg to look over their storehouse. I loved the section with only sofas, as well as the many varieties of tables and chairs, and the place where brass chandeliers were kept. A feeling of happiness streamed through me. The storehouse had the air of a giant junk shop. The assorted furniture looked at me and told me stories: about the people who had made them, and about those people with whom they had spent decades as silent guests. I sniffed at parlor cupboards and buffets, just as I snoop around in old cellars where dusty objects, gathered or forgotten over generations, age in silence. To me, moldy air is like Chanel No. 5.

Although the film people were enthusiastic about my authentic scenery, they did not treat their own furniture with the proper respect. They scratched the top of a beautiful piano by moving a bust of Beethoven back and forth across it. Instead of putting new veneer on such a valuable piece, they got brown floor paint to fix it. Another time, they drove ten-inch screws through a buffet. My heart bled.

"Guys, none of the paneling is screwed on right," I tried to tell them, but only got annoyed looks. So I got down to work myself and gave the sideboard its proper appearance.

In the movie *The Undignified Crone*, which was partly filmed in my museum, Hanne Hiob, Bertold Brecht's daughter, played the lead. I had prepared a room for her to rest in between takes. But at one point, some scenes had to be shot even there. Where could she go? Since the entire house was being used as a movie set, I had set up my brass bed in the toilet. I quickly offered Hanne Hiob my bed. She gladly accepted my offer and thanked me in her straightforward and unassuming way.

Whatever I earned in fees, I put back into "my" house. I procured lime, stones, and cement, paid the workers, and bought new furniture. In the first few years, I worked like a horse. What I built up, working with my bare hands, is now worth three hundred thousand marks. In 1972, the DDR government expressed its first, and of course also its last, recognition of all my labor: the house was designated a historic monument.

My first small role in a film was in a piece on the life of Ludwig von Beethoven. I was a violin maker. In my second movie, *On the Way to Atlantis*, I played a lady at a ball, a role I got through sheer accident. My first scene as an officer in uniform—a role I performed against my will—had been filmed, when the director's assistant began to run up and down, wildly gesticulating with his hands. He seemed to be in great difficulty. The film took place at the court of Queen Victoria and for the next scene he needed a line of courtiers. But the women from the Friedrichstadt Palace, engaged to dance with them, had left him in the lurch. The assistant was beside himself, but his face relaxed when he came up with an idea. He fixed his eyes on me, grinning with expectation, "You, get to the wardrobe and into costume." He didn't have to say it twice because this role was made for me. I didn't *play* the lady at court, I *was* the lady at court.

At that time, Tutti and I would occasionally go to the few remaining bars where gays and lesbians could meet: the Goldschmidt Bar or the City-Klause on Friedrichstrasse. We tried to make the best of these dismal conditions. But more than once, while walking through the area in drag, we noticed that as transvestites we were a minority within a minority.

One time, the bitch sitting next to me in the City-Klause was showing off some crocheted thing she was proudly holding up, boasting, "I made this." It was clearly supposed to be a purse—very amateurish work. At some point, she turned on me, her eyes angry slits in her fishy face, "Make yourself scarce, you blond goat. You have no business at this table."

You stupid slut, you can go jump in the lake, I thought. I picked up my purse and punished her by ignoring her. Friends at another table started calling to me, "Lottchen, our Lottchen is here. Come, there's room for you here." That made Miss Born-to-Be-Cheap look like the stupid sow she was.

Chapter 19

IN THE SIXTIES, THE STASI paid their first visit to my museum: two men, not tall, not stout, with the piercing eyes of birds of prey, in patent leather coats. I offered them chairs. I also sat down, had to sit down, because I was close to fainting with apprehension and would have collapsed otherwise, although I was not guilty of anything.

But they had not come to take my museum away, not yet. The government's Bureau for the Commerce in Fine Arts had cast its greedy eye on the automated music player and record collection, the latter consisting of about fifteen thousand pieces that had come to me from the Scheunenviertel through my friend, the collector Alfred Kirschner.

DDR laws gave every pretext for "legal" expropriation, and as early as the end of the sixties, the Bureau for the Commerce in Fine Arts in the Frankfurt Allée in Berlin sold on the black market for foreign money everything that was not nailed down. Furniture, paintings, clocks, carpets, glassware, porcelains, museum and church properties, all were cleaned out to arrest the economic bankruptcy of the DDR. Later on, the predatory raids expanded to even include paving stones, coaches, locomotives, and old cars. And if old houses could have been carted away and rebuilt, many a baroque mansion would today be standing in the USA. In containers and freight trains, the cultural heritage of the DDR was dissipated across the border over a period of twenty years.

Alfred Kirschner, who had collected automated music players, gramophones, music boxes, and records since he was six years old, was one of the most lovable human beings I have ever met.

His short body almost always in motion, as if he didn't want to suffer even a moment of repose, this whirlwind of a man was one of the pleasant people who, although blessed with many talents, wasn't interested in impressing anyone. He also paid no attention to his appearance. He always wore a spotted, well-worn suit, usually with a checkered shirt underneath, the ever-present leather or fabric cap aslant on his head. Appearances didn't matter to him at all, as if in fighting for survival he had long ago learned to slough off all petty vanities, if he had ever been subject to them.

Alfred Kirschner was a musical genius, a piano virtuoso. If asked, he would play every conceivable piece of music from classics to popular songs. I remember a ball where he was playing Liszt's "Hungarian Rhapsody" and Rossini's "William Tell Overture" to great effect. Out of the blue, a young man requested, "Adelheid, play the 'Gartenzwerg'," a still well-known, simple German ballad. Alfred looked up at the ceiling and sniffed with his pointed nose as if to suck the melody from the air; the notes seemed to gather in his head, and he quickly started to play the "Zwerg" song.

Another time, I had sent out invitations to a celebration in my museum in the hall overlooking the garden. Many people had gathered, including Alfred. Margaret, my loyal assistant—together we had pounded about ten thousand stones for the house in twenty years—inserted a music roll into the German pianola at the left window and called out, "And now, ladies and gentlemen, the 'Waldeslust.' " Alfred had in the meantime taken a seat at the American piano, made by Steck of New York, that stood at the right window. As soon as the first notes sounded from the automatic pianola, Alfred accompanied it live. It was a wonderful concert of mechanical and manual piano, since the differences in wood yielded different sounds from each instrument, resulting in delicate nuances of tone. The American piano had a sharper tone than the German one, and the audience was enchanted. When the final sounds died away, the applause was long and enthusiastic.

Alfred was caught in the claws of the Stasi for selling pieces of his collection to Westerners, not to enrich himself, but to obtain other items. The court sentenced him to years in prison and a large fine as a currency profiteer. Since he could not pay the fine—he was a man of limited means—his apartment was emptied before his eyes. And how! While their Stasi colleagues were pulling his linen out of the chest and throwing it on the floor, the furniture packers from the Bureau for the Commerce in Fine Arts were already waiting at the door. Music boxes, clocks, automated music players, gathered by him with love and passion, disappeared into the insatiable maw of those receivers of stolen goods. They left him only his wretched bedstead. They broke Alfred Kirschner's will to live. He vegetated a few more years in a Protestant nursing home in Weissensee and then died. When I visited him for the last time, he had turned into an old man with sparse, disheveled gray hair whose eyes could no longer make the effort to look up.

Both Stasi representatives in my museum were in a hurry. One, casting his eyes back and forth between a list and objects on display, pointed with a thin index finger at specific gramophones, music boxes, and automatic music players. Alfred Kirschner had given them to the museum years ago. Against the will of the donor, who wanted these collector's items preserved for the public, the real currency profiteers moved everything marked down on their lists into the furniture van that they had, with practical foresight, brought along. For me, the inscription "K & A" on their elegant truck never stood for "Kunst & Antiquitäten" [Art & Antiquities] but meant "Klau & Ausverkauf" [Claw & Sell-out] instead.

In August 1973, the head of the recently founded Art and Antiquities Limited/International Company for the Export and Import of Works of Art, Horst Schuster, appeared with his entourage. He was a correctly dressed nouveau riche who with pompous gestures and an important air handed me his visiting card like someone who needed this token of his worth and influence because he at least suspected that his talents were only average and nothing but chance had pushed him to the top. He made me a fantastic offer: that sterile businessman wanted to buy my entire museum for the art trade. He offered me two hundred thousand tax-free marks, and an executive position in the art trade center that the mansion would be converted into. Customers from other countries would be brought through these large rooms to view the objects on display. Business would then be done in the office. Barracks would be erected in the park according to Schuster's painstaking plan. My museum had been selected to take over the function which was later held by Mühlenbeck near Oranienburg: an elegant antique salon and center of "Art & Antiquities Limited," one of twelve export firms in Schalck-Golodkowskis empire of "Commercial Coordination."

"Look, for me these things are alive. I haven't collected them to do business with them, but because I found them beautiful."

The gentlemen, who obviously thought their offer more than fair, could not understand that kind of attitude. They left in a sullen mood, letting me know that they had other choices. Something was in the air, particularly after a museum expert, suppressing his amazement with difficulty as I gave him a tour of the rooms, judged that my pieces represented the most important Historismus collection in all of Europe.

In November, I promptly received a summons to appear at the city council's finance department. The official gruffly informed me that I owed property taxes. They had abruptly decided to consider the sum that the objects in the museum were insured for as the value of the property and demanded ten thousand marks in back taxes from me. And how was I, living on my sparse DEFA income and the voluntary donations of the visitors to the museum, to pay this astronomical sum? The answer given by the finance bureaucrat was: Sell. Naturally, to Art and Antiquities Limited.

The tax department became a willing accomplice in the sell-out of cultural treasures by the DDR. Beginning in the seventies, they brought "refractory" collectors to see "reason" in order to deprive them of their possessions. Since owning private property was disapproved of by officials of the DDR, collectors were automatically suspect. The SED government only saw the monetary value of each object as "inciting to fraud"; they did not see that most collectors did not think of making money with their passion. Their greatest reward was in the contemplation of these objects. They would often lend their works of art to museums, so that interested visitors could share this pleasure, or left their treasures to a foundation, knowing that their life's work would be in good hands.

The looting of these objects from collectors always followed the same scheme. The assessors of Art and Antiquities Limited would examine the collection, pronounce a drastic increase in value—completely unrealistic for the lovers of old objects since they, unlike the official company, could not sell their goods on a Western market—and would then send their expert findings to the local finance bureau. Based on these ridiculous figures, the finance department in turn calculated an enormous profit on these items for which taxes were due—even when, for example, the appraised baroque cabinet had not changed hands for decades. The debtors could not pay, since they had never earned money with their collections, and the truck from Art and Antiquities Limited would immediately be at their doors.

Hidden under the cover of reasonable tax laws was nothing but expropriation without compensation. Often the preparations for the "disposal" were finalized before the preliminary inquiry had been established.

Chapter 20

On February 1, 1974, the Department of Culture and Monuments held a hearing at which the fate of my museum was to be decided. Manfred Maurer, with whom I had already had a bad experience in the Märkische Museum, took over the hearing. Only the state could run my house as a museum; besides, according to ordinance 11/47 of August 10, 1972, a museum cannot be privately owned. In "our state," Maurer continued, I was not fit to be in charge of a museum since I was in no position to produce the appropriate credentials either politically or culturally.

The gentlemen did not want to acknowledge that without my two hands it would all be a wasteland, that nothing would have been created here if I were not a woman in a man's body. Because as a child I had played with doll furniture, because I am still a neat housewife today, because Gründerzeit amuses me, and because I always want a home around me: that's why the museum stands.

The gentlemen were well prepared. Their plan was for me to sell everything to the state. As a lawyer informed me the next day, I would not only have gotten rid of my entire collection, including my bedstead, I would also have had to pay four thousand five hundred and eighty-two marks in taxes.

I refused to sign on the spot as Maurer demanded in a snarling voice, but instead obtained the cited paragraphs—a laborious undertaking that took weeks since one could not easily gain access to legal texts in the DDR: citizens were deprived of their rights by making it impossible for them to know their rights. I was amazed when I turned to the page that contained ordinance 11/47: the decree had nothing to do with the right to run a museum, but dealt with regulations on fishing. They had deliberately misled me.

Is this the end of my life's work, my life's purpose? I asked myself the evening of February first. The floor had been pulled out from under me. I felt like a tree whose roots had been severed. I spent a sleepless night sitting on the edge of my bed. Then I ran through the rooms, got an axe from the cellar, and made up my mind to chop up all the furniture, throw it out the window, and bring it to my mother in a cart. As firewood, it would at least serve some purpose. But I couldn't bring myself to do it.

The next morning, my co-worker looked at me in shock, "My God, look at you!" I thought, *My hair hasn't been combed, but how could it be disheveled if I haven't gone to bed?* I looked in the mirror—my hair had turned white overnight. That outward change, an image of my inner state, did not bother me. It all seemed as far away as the rocks on the moon. The only important thing was the museum.

Suddenly an idea came into my head: if there is nothing, the Stasi can't take anything away and the authorities lose their power to commit an injustice. I made my horrible choice. I would give everything away to the visitors at my museum, and the fine gentlemen from the art trade would find an empty shack. That I might be put in jail for sabotage didn't matter to me.

From little side rooms and the attic, my storehouse, I dragged everything into the show rooms. I arranged eighty-six oil lamps on the extension table in the Neo-Gothic dining room. In the Neo-Renaissance living room, on a table at which twenty people could be seated, I spread sixty-four chimney clocks, and next to them, I put all kinds of timepieces: brass and bronze anniversary clocks; elegant gilded clocks from a palace, next to a cheap one from a workman's family, with a balance and a screwed-on eagle made of pressed molten zinc.

Also distributed around the room: the largest cohesive collection of Edison phonograph rolls in the world, fifteen thousand pieces; thirty-three standing clocks and three hundred eighty-six regulators; eighteen pianos and buffets; my sewing machine and music box collections; porcelain, cutlery, glassware; thirteen thousand records, more than three thousand pianola rolls and the accompanying parts; the chair collection, bedroom, dining room, study and salon chairs, benches for sitting near stoves, tavern, kitchen and children's chairs, altogether more than sixty pieces—everything went, as did my inventory of tables. Through the decades, I had collected complete sets of furniture for twenty-three rooms.

How was I able to gather such an enormous amount under "socialism"? I often received more bequests than I had room for. At the beginning of the fifties, for example, I got to know old Mrs. Barnewitz through a colleague at the Märkische Museum. Berta Barnewitz led me through her apartment with solemn gravity and showed me the old pieces made in 1892 by the master carpenter Julius Groschkus in Berlin. A magnificent buffet with columns and carvings stood hidden in the corner of a windowless connecting room, but without its top structure.

Where was it? Berta Barnewitz pointed to the cellar door, "The coal cellar is really dirty." I felt my way down by candlelight and discovered something covered in black dust in the furthest corner: the top to the buffet, with only one of its wooden globes missing. I rooted around in the coals until I found it. Berta Barnewitz was not at all delighted when I placed the cleaned top on the buffet, but shook her delicately shaped head thoughtfully. Of small stature, she was never able to keep those dust-collecting embellishments clean. I promised to appear with a feather duster every four weeks. When she passed away, I managed to obtain her furniture at the last minute from the executor and brought it to my museum in Mahlsdorf.

"The museum is dead. Take your pick," I told the surprised visitors one day soon after the proceedings at city hall. Crowds of people ran out with the treasures they had grabbed, loading the more bulky items on their car trailers or rented furniture trucks.

Three months later, with three-quarters of my collection gone, I noticed a young woman eagerly taking notes as I led the visitors through what was left of my museum. At first, I thought it meant more bullying by the Stasi. But in her jeans and plain sweater, she looked too modest for someone from Normannenstrasse. "It's disgusting what they are doing to you," the woman with the open face said angrily after my "tour of the remnants." She handed me her card: Annekathrin Burger, Actress. "You need a good lawyer."

"Mrs. Burger, that is very kind of you, but no lawyer would stick his neck out for my old furniture."

"Oh, yes, there is one," she said, "Mr. Kaul. I know him well."

Professor Dr. Karl-Friedrich Kaul, the world famous showpiece of DDR jurisprudence, would concern himself with my museum? I could not believe such a silver lining on my horizon. But the next day the telephone rang. A calm but important-sounding voice said, "This is Kaul. I've been told you have some problems. When can you come to see me? Today? Tomorrow? The day after?"

"If you can't pay the tax," the man in charge of the finance department had said, smiling spitefully, "then we'll confiscate the pieces. And you know how little they are worth in the pawnshop on Wilhelm-Pieck Strasse." Like a sword of Damocles, the threat of seizure hung on a silken thread over my head. I went to see Kaul at once.

Enthroned behind a huge, oaken desk, an older man sat with his mighty hands propped against the table like a Jewish patriarch. Despite his impassive expression, his face appeared thoughtful and almost preoccupied. But as I told my story, his cheeks reddened. As soon as I finished, he ran his fingers through his light hair and adjusted his eyeglasses. He angrily banged his flat hand on some legal briefs lying in front of him so that letters flew up like frightened doves from the table; he thundered, "When that happens, it will by my last day as a lawyer in this state!" He rang for his secretary. She was barely at the door when he called out to her, his face flushed with fury, "Take two letters—one to the Minister of Finance and one to the Minister of Culture."

During this bizarre drama, my glance had fallen on the mullioned Art Nouveau windows and I began to feel a glimmer of hope. While dictating, Kaul stalked back and forth in the room, like a tiger in his cage. The old-fashioned office furniture, the comfortable chaos—I suddenly felt content and secure!

"Have you already paid any taxes?"

"Yes, three hundred marks."

He leaped from the chair where he had in the meantime sat down. His right hand flew up; pointing his index finger at me, he shouted, "You'll get them back!"

His attentive old-maid secretary in her beige outfit seemed utterly overwhelmed by his display of temper and looked alternately at Kaul and at me as if she were following the ball in a game of tennis.

Kaul explained that it would take time. "But don't worry, I'll get those taxes canceled."

It took until June 1976, but I then had it in black and white: I no longer owed property taxes. When I asked Kaul what his fee was, he grandly waved it aside, "You owe me absolutely nothing; on the contrary, I wish you and your museum the best."

Everywhere—even in the former DDR—there were and are pleasant and less pleasant, clean and somewhat dirtier people, rascals and idiots, but also good and wise people. There are always men of questionable character. At important moments, I often had the good fortune to meet people who meant well and who did not go along with the unjust regime. Thanks to the selfless lawyer Kaul, God bless him, and Annekathrin Burger, my museum lived on and did not become a devastated ruin.

Many items did not interest the visitors even for free. Three buffets with columns that needed restoring, one Art Nouveau, one Neo-Renaissance from about 1890, both made of walnut, and one from the 1870's made of oak, were untouched; also left were one Art Nouveau piano and three in Neo-Renaissance style which, according to a maker of such instruments, could only be restored at a huge cost—as well as worm-infested kitchen cabinets and damaged chairs. Since these items would have been assessed for the insurance on the house, I had to reduce them to firewood. The big chunks, columns and moldings, locks and metal fittings, I salvaged for extra parts.

When the museum was saved in 1976, the remaining collection consisted of: an oak Neo-Gothic dining room, factory-made around 1900; a living room with a piano in Neo-Renaissance style from 1890, also factory-made; a hunting room in Neo-Renaissance style produced in 1892, with hand-carved sculptures of oak from the Spessart region; a ladies' sitting room from the year 1891, the furnishings for a garden room and a dining room from 1892 and a bedroom from the year 1880 from Leipzig—all made of American walnut and finished in Neo-Renaissance style; the complete set of my great-uncle's modest Neo-Renaissance living room furniture from 1895, also made of American walnut in Karlsruhe. In addition, there were some single pieces which due to a lack of space were standing in the foyer; what remained of my clock, music box and picture collections; a complete set of furnishings for a kitchen from 1890 Berlin; and naturally, from the same year, the Neo-Renaissance furnishings of the Mulackritze, in painted pine, and the public room that came with it; a small, private kitchen with simple furniture from 1875, which was not open to the public; and for filming, two kitchen sets from 1870 and 1900 and a Neo-Renaissance, American walnut bedroom, also used as a prop, manufactured in 1883.

The few salvaged parts for clocks, music boxes, phonographs, gramophones, and automated music players accompanied chandeliers for candles or oil, as well as stoves and curtains that went with each room, and rugs, some of them very worn. Last but not least, there was the heavy granite memorial plaque commemorating the birth of Prince August von Preussen on September 19, 1779 at the Friedrichsfelde Palace.

It was through sheer chance that all this remained, although I would have fought tooth and nail to protect my uncle's heirlooms and the furnishings of the Mulackritze from anyone who came too close.

Chapter 21

"You have such a large circle of friends. We'd like you to write down the names of your visitors." Both gentlemen from the "Listen and Look Company"—they almost always appeared in pairs—presented their request in a sly-friendly manner.

I smiled pleasantly, "Oh, there are so many people who hang around here, probably more than a hundred. I know most of them by first name only and I certainly don't have their addresses."

"How come?" they both asked in unison.

"Good God, don't you know, that comes from Nazi days—for safety reasons."

They exchanged a malicious look and tried a different tack. "Couldn't you inconspicuously take down the license numbers of your visitors?" And after a short pause, "Tell me, do you own a car?"

"No, only a bicycle."

"Don't you want to buy a car?"

I began to suspect something fishy. Are they going to offer me one in exchange for giving them information? "No, I am much too slow to drive a car. My reaction time is just good enough for bicycling. Driving a car, I'd hit the nearest tree."

Slimy, half-hearted laughter from the gentlemen from Stasi.

The SED government rigorously rejected homosexuality until late into the eighties. They behaved as if we didn't exist. Bars were closed or put under observation, we were not allowed to advertise in the personal columns—even in the Kaiser's time people were more open-minded in this regard—and so we could only meet each other in teahouses, parks, or private parties.

If we gave a party in the museum, state security was part of the group. A friend conspiratorially pulled me into the kitchen at one of these parties and handed me a note, "The man with the dark beard sitting under the movie poster works for the Stasi."

Well, he's not the only one, I thought, *I'm not going to let him spoil the fun.* With that, the case was closed as far as I was concerned.

"Five years ago, we began our work," announced the Homosexual

Interest Group of Berlin in the *Mahlsdorfer Homo-Info*. One of the first gay-lesbian initiatives in the DDR, the group celebrated its founding in January 1978. We didn't suspect, as we listened to the gramophone music in the Mulackritze, that it would be the last anniversary.

But taking things in their turn. It was in 1974, I believe, that a scientific talk on homosexuality was given at the East Berlin Library. I descended the stairs afterwards deep in thought. As I stepped outside, I could hear a jumble of voices. On the street, men and women were making themselves heard, encouraging each other in a kind of pantomime: What is our life like? Forbidden to gather, no possibility of advertising.

I stood aside for a while and followed the discussion. Then I walked over and suggested to them, "Well, if you're looking for meeting rooms, you can come to my house in Mahlsdorf. You need not pay rent, only a little something for electricity and heat."

Thus we began to have talks and to meet each other in the museum, with state security suspecting the worst conspiratorial activities going on at our meetings.

We crowded into the Mulackritze. Up to fifty people sat on the bar, on the floor, or squeezed onto the window seat. I converted the cellar next to it into rooms for dancing and a lecture hall—*jour fixe*. Lesbian mothers, gay fathers, simple working men and women, actors, engineers, doctors: all met in the Mulackritze.

Whoever did not want to have serious talks amused himself in the dance hall. We were like a family, particularly for those who had been cast off by their own families. The sensitive among such outlaws often shed bitter tears when we celebrated their birthdays. We comforted them in our arms.

But there was not always a happy ending. An angel of a child, eighteen or nineteen, Sylvia was her name, suddenly stopped coming to our meetings. *Where could she be?* we wondered. Until someone found out the painful truth. Sylvia had taken her own life. Driven out long ago by her mother and declared a persona non grata, she saw no other way out of her loneliness. It is that easy to destroy such delicate souls.

I called the mother to offer my condolences, to hear her voice, perhaps hoping to do some good, to get some small spark of understanding from her for the "depraved" daughter. But the mother only shouted, "Are you one too?"

I hung up. There is no worse sickness than human ignorance and intolerance.

Our goal was to give gays and lesbians a center for communicating, and to be able to live openly as homosexuals following Rosa von

Praunheim's maxim, "It is not the homosexual who is perverse, but the society which condemns him." Some members of our interest group had seen a film on Western television that dealt with a new acceptance of gays and lesbians in the DDR. But many did not have the endurance, and looked for a way to go west.

There is some consolation in saying good-bye, in embracing at the train station, even if the parting may be forever. There was a dreadful strangeness in the way those who left or were deported were simply gone one day. You may have spoken to them only yesterday, but they gave no hint, could not give any hint of what was going on inside them. There was no farewell between friends.

It was really hard on the feminine men who wanted to avoid the army at any price. I knew some who, because they knew of no way out, chose the most drastic solution. They turned on the gas.

The homosexual women wanted to hold a meeting of lesbians at my place in April of 1978. They sent invitations throughout the DDR, which became known to state security. The German post office usually did a little more than just deliver letters. Sometimes they saved the recipient the labor of reading them.

One day before the meeting, two policemen rang my doorbell. One, all prim and proper, had put on a condescendingly calm official expression, while the other, amused at my outfit, regarded me with a supercilious, jeering look. Prim-and-Proper came right to the point and driveled something about a forbidden event.

"I'm only inviting some guests."

"What kind of guests are they?"

"Gay girls like me. Why all these questions?"

Had I posted a placard saying, "Lesbians of the DDR are meeting for a dance and discussion at the Mahlsdorf Gründerzeit Museum"? No, I had not. But that made no impression on him.

"You are ill acquainted with the laws of the German Democratic Republic," he lectured me. If more than six people get together, even for Uncle Otto's birthday, it becomes an event that the police must approve. I should hang a sign at the door saying, "Event canceled due to a broken water pipe." I declined to do so.

There was great consternation among the organizers. The police had already questioned some of them and seemed particularly interested in knowing whether women from West Berlin had been invited. The what-do-we-do-now frame of mind did not last long. Whereas gays would probably have run around like excited chickens, the lesbians came up with a plan that could have been devised by the staff of a general.

Since it was too late to notify any of the guests, they drummed up all the members of the Berlin group and gathered at the train station the next day. There, they stopped the unsuspecting women from going to my place and directed them to a secret meeting place instead. Naturally, not all of them could be caught in time; a few ended up knocking at my door. But a few minutes later, the lesbians drove up with squealing tires, took charge of the startled women, and off they went. The meeting took place after all.

A few days later, I received a letter from the Bureau of Culture, "Herewith Lothar Berfelde has been denied all permits to hold meetings or gatherings at the Gründerzeit Museum."

That regulation was not directed against meetings of gays and lesbians only. The workers' brigades, which had in the meantime adopted tours of the Gründerzeit Museum in their cultural program, were forbidden to move into the more homey part after their tour: a visit to the irreplaceable Mulackritze had been crossed off.

Chapter 22

My quarrel with government offices over my museum continued, even though the eighties had begun with so much promise. Two ladies from the housing department were extremely enthusiastic, "Mr. Berfelde, you've made a museum out of this house! We were going to tear it down. And even today, there isn't much we can do with it. Wouldn't you like to buy the house?"

"How can I?"

They offered it to me at no charge. I was overjoyed. But I should have learned something from the delays and uncertainties of the sixties and seventies. Firm declarations were followed by—nothing.

The announced assessor never came. The magistrate in charge of the Department of People's Property remained evasive and put me off. Once, I was told that no estate houses were for sale. "My dear sir," I said to the man handling the case, "this house hasn't been an estate house since 1920. I don't know whether you're selling me an old village school or a kindergarten, but in any case, an estate house you're definitely not selling me. The fact remains that you would be signing over a condemned ruin out of which I made something." The man looked at me out of his slanted eyes as though I were from another star.

Two years later, new members from the Department of Community Housing appeared, this time with the chief. I was told to fill out another purchase form like the one in 1982. Soon after came the news that I was a single person and thus not authorized to live in so many rooms. What nonsense! Almost all the rooms are part of the museum; even my bedroom, which has a painted porcelain chamber pot under the bed, is open to visitors.

State security went on probing. They were probably asking themselves, "Could this beastly Lieschen be talked into selling furniture to the West?"

Even in the early eighties, visitors from abroad, mainly from France and England, found their way to Mahlsdorf. I continued to be surprised at how international the public that appeared at the museum was, since I had no way of knowing where in the world articles about the museum had been published, in what books or reference works on museums, antique dealers or collections Mahlsdorf had been mentioned. After Netherlands television came to the museum from Amsterdam, it did not take long for whole school groups to arrive in buses from Holland.

Obviously state security became aware of the situation and set a trap for me. One day an "American," very blond, very agile, lips thin as wires and painted bright red, came tripping up the steps. She had parked her huge sled with a US license plate in full view. The blonde—she really looked as American as a Stasi Central-made artwork—rushed from one room to the next, waxing more and more euphoric. "What cost? I buy and pay in dollar! What cost, what cost?" she kept shouting enthusiastically in affected slang.

"My dear lady," I began, but she would not let me say a word and started to bargain, as if she were in an Oriental bazaar. The only difference was that she seemed ready to pay any price. She behaved like Rockefeller's mistress. At a certain point, I had enough and I interrupted her avalanche of words. "Whether you have a lot of money or very little doesn't matter to me. This is not an old-furniture market, but a museum, and I have nothing to sell. 'Watching' only!"

"Oh," she said, with badly acted disappointment. I mustn't be too hasty, but should think it over. "Too bad, too bad, too bad." She came a second time. Had I done otherwise, I am sure I would have shared the fate of my friend Alfred Kirschner.

I had planted a piece of land belonging to the museum like the grounds of an old estate. Rural and natural, it seemed like a little forest. An idyll—until 1987.

That the socialist bureaucracy had no understanding of the true value and beauty of things had already occurred to me. But what the Hellersdorf Bureau of Gardens arranged to celebrate the 750th anniversary of Berlin had a new quality. Great things were being planned. Workmen came streaming forth to make it happen. In the wake of the "reconstruction" declared by the Bureau of Gardens, the Mahlsdorf estate grounds were to become a socialist greensward.

One hundred fifty-two trees were cut down. The park became a desert. Every elderberry and lilac bush was flattened by men with machines gone wild. Right after that, they excavated fifty centimeters of topsoil and scattered some worthless rubble from the Ahrensfeld building project on top in its place. The undertaking was planned with such expertise that even today the walls get soaked from excess run-off whenever it rains. The furniture in the cellar is starting to disintegrate. The house is decaying.

"Leave at least this one poplar standing for memory's sake," I pleaded. It was taller than the house. But there was no talking to those apes. A quarter of an hour later, there was the screech of an electric saw and the glorious tree fell over. The heavy machinery killed seven eagles. Deer, guinea-fowls, pheasants, and rare birds such as owls disappeared forever.

The Hellersdorf administration proudly announced the creation of a Biedermeiergarden—a category for which one would search through books on the history of art in vain.

Chapter 23

IN 1988, I CAME OF "TRAVELING AGE" like every sixty-year old citizen of the DDR. To be sure, I was not pensioned because the SED government realized that I was a woman, but because a doctor certified that I was entitled to it.

I can clearly recall my first border crossing. "Come in," the border official urged. I was wearing long pants and a coat because it was very cold. "Open your coat. What have you got in the inside pockets?"

"The coat doesn't have any inside pockets, it's a ladies' coat."

"Turn around and raise your coat. What do you have in the back pants pockets?"

"My pants don't have any pockets in the back. They are ladies' pants."

"And what have you got in the front pockets?"

"These pants don't have any front pockets either."

The uniformed official with his moist moon face looked so foolish at that point, that I felt triumphant: Serves you right, you crud. He, of course, went over every centimeter of my handbag with extra care, "What kind of photos are these?"

"Those are pictures of the interior of my Gründerzeit Museum."

When he came upon the picture of me in a dress and wig, standing at the sideboard, he asked, "Is that you?"

"Yes, and you can come see that sideboard and the whole museum for free any Sunday."

He never came.

In the spring of 1988, a week before the opening of their Gründerzeit collection, I went to the Cultural Foundation at Britz Palace in West Berlin. Both of my colleagues at the Berlin museum, entrusted with putting together the collection, had looked me up in 1984 to "spy" on me as they jokingly said. "Yes," I replied, delighted that the Gründerzeit would have a second museum in Berlin, "spy all you want, I'll be happy to tell you how a housewife furnished her home in 1880."

"We're glad you've come because we still have some questions," the museum experts greeted me as I arrived at Britz Palace. They pointed to two bronze candlesticks, "Do they fit into the style of the era?"

"Perfectly! They're Neo-Renaissance, 1880, with scrolls, interlaced spirals. Yes, these are just right here, like the ones they had at the time."

"If we only knew who made them," they wondered, puzzled. They had purchased these two good pieces in an antique shop where nobody could tell them.

"No problem," I informed them, "Stobwasser & Company, Berlin Bronze and Zincware Factory, in Berlin C on Wallstrasse."

A standing clock, with columns and balustrade, stood in a corner. I was delighted to be in my element, "Oh, yes, Gustav Becker, Clockmaker, Freiburg in Schlesien. This one was made in 1900, walnut, veneered, and alder. Only the hands have been replaced, they are Art Nouveau, and the top is missing." I stood on tip-toe, felt around on the ledge, and sure enough, I could feel the dowel holes where the top had previously been attached. Both of them laughed, and went to get some paper in order to write down my comments. When it comes to things like that, I am a walking furniture catalogue, but woe is me should anyone ask what I had for lunch yesterday.

Chapter 24

SHORTLY AFTER THIS EXPERIENCE, while I was outside cleaning the doormat and the front steps, two "gentlemen" came marching up. Without any greeting, they showed their I.D.'s. "Is this the private museum?" "Yes."

"We're looking for Citizen Berfelde. Is that you by any chance?"

I was standing on the steps like a cleaning woman, wearing an apron and kerchief, whisk broom and dustpan in my hands, and answered, "Yes, that's me. I've collected it all from childhood on, and since August 1, 1960, the museum is open to everyone free of charge."

The one in the trench coat thundered, "To us, you are an undesirable person, remember that."

"It's a good thing that I know that now, gentlemen," I answered and curtsied.

Trying to look important, they exchanged a long look. Then they abruptly turned, marched down the steps like tin soldiers, and disappeared without any farewell. That was the Stasi's last visit to me. They wanted to frighten me one more time, so that I would stay in West Berlin the next time I went "abroad." My co-worker would have been kicked out, the furniture truck for the transportation of art would have driven up and carted everything away.

These Stasi-Johns behaved like big shots, but seemed more like two puppets in their pompous demeanor. "We have the power and you are a zero," was their message. Their puffed-up masquerade simply amused me.

"30 years of DDR—30 years of the State Circus" read the sign on the winter quarters of the state circus in Hoppegarten. The zealous single-minded workers in the propaganda department of the SED government supplied us with unintended comedy: "Let everyone come out on May first!" This watchword had been affixed by a well-meaning but obviously simple-minded propaganda group to the walls of a cemetery.

The slogans for the most important holiday of the year, May first, were still there in the middle of the month, and the exhortations to celebrate the founding day were still up on October seventh and into the beginning of November, as if even the authorities themselves doubted the durability of their creation.

We should guard against equating the DDR dictatorship with National Socialism. It is possible to draw comparisons—and there are parallels—if they serve to help our understanding. But one thing is certain: The assembly line murder of millions of people from 1933 to 1945 by the Germans remains a gruesome exception, against which any other comparison becomes invalid.

My admiration and sympathy go to all those who wanted to make socialist ideas a reality, but failed, were doomed to fail because of the inadequacy of human beings. The idea remains a good one, even when discredited by the reality of socialism.

I only became aware of the agony of this socialism, which was not true socialism, with the building of the wall. A state that has to lock up its citizens in order to survive cannot last. Its downfall became clear to me when the Department of Culture for the Marzahn district called me up with a bizarre request: I was to evaluate the furniture that the so-called "people going abroad" wanted to take to the West with them. The museums of the DDR, whose employees usually handled this delicate task, could no longer keep up with the great number of people wanting to leave.

If these "tourists"—out of sheer spite I always called them "emigrants" even in front of officials since tourists usually return, something these people had no intention of doing—wanted to take any household goods along, they had to list every single item, even underwear and washcloths, and submit five to seven copies of the list, depending on the degree of chicanery of the district. This was to let them know for the last time who was in power here and what dirt they all were.

With my new job, I entered dangerous territory. I began with the intention of overturning the very meaning and purpose of the exercise which was to ferret out any valuable antiques hidden in the households of the travelers. If the state could export art works every day, then the people who were leaving because they were being tormented here should at least have the right, damn it, to take their personal possessions along!

My first appraisal took place in Kaulsdorf in the home of a musician. To my horror I noticed a cupboard of peasant design from the year 1820 and next to it an oak chest with the date 1786 worked into it. What should I do? "How am I supposed to assess this?" I asked my colleague from the Office of Cultural Affairs, pointing at the chest and cupboard.

"Oh, it's all very simple," she chattered blithely, "category I, II, or III."

"Just what is meant by category I, II, or III?"

Consternation appeared on her face. "Oh, I've just been given the task of accompanying you to these appraisals," she said with a helpless smile, "I don't know that either." A harmless rabbit, untroubled by any professional knowledge. *If this is how the state is run, then it won't be long before the collapse,* I thought, and was satisfied. To clear up the question of categories, I telephoned the Märkische Museum. I described the cupboard and chest to my colleague, the "furniture aunt" of the establishment.

"Category I comprises international works of art which are not to be exported, for example, a Rembrandt or a Rubens. But nobody has those," she slyly added. "Category II signifies national artifacts which extends to works by living artists of the DDR. These can be exported, but only with the approval of the Ministry of Culture, while category III represents local artifacts, which means pieces from the industrial era, the Gründerzeit and Art Nouveau, unless they are unusual items, such as a desk by van de Velde." The cupboard and chest, since there were an abundance of them in the DDR museums, I assigned to category III.

The number of those prepared to turn their backs on this government under any circumstance rose so steeply from the mid-eighties on, that I was working all over East Berlin. One day, I was standing in a man's apartment stuffed with antiques: pewter plates, candlesticks, paintings. I closed one eye and assigned them to category III. However, in the house of this frightened-looking man, it became necessary to close both eyes.

I found myself staring in amazement at a valuable war chest from the sixteenth century, but in the style of the middle ages, which had been perfectly restored by an expert and which he claimed was his possession. I would have preferred seeing that piece dirtied inside and out to give it a better chance of getting through.

"Who restored this piece?" I asked, and when the owner named the Museum of German History, I sat down on a stool in dismay. "Oh, shit," escaped me.

A conspiratorial conversation then ensued. After all, one never knows to whom one is talking. "You want to take this chest with you?"

"Yes."

"You're quite sure?"

"Yes."

"Are you very attached to this chest?"

"Yes, otherwise I would not have had it restored."

"Who did the restoration?"

He gave a name, and I asked, "Do you know this man?"

"Yes."

"Do you know this man very well?"

"Yes."

"Is he reliable?"

"Yes, a hundred percent."

We put everything on one card, and on the list of assessments I wrote, "One iron chest with various locks, about 1900," and furthermore, "The entries listed here belong in category III, local items, and do not fall under the Artwork Protection Regulations of the DDR. No objections to their export. I pressed the stamp onto the pad—bang—stamped "Mahlsdorf Museum" on it, then my signature, beautifully legible. The crate went through.

Another time, a family with whom I had arranged a secret message called from Hamburg, "All of us are healthy. The journey was beautiful." That meant: Everything had gone well, the furniture withstood the border crossing and the transport.

Since many travelers were unaware that everything, up to their last shirt, had to have an authorization to be allowed across the border, and that customs mercilessly sent those who lacked the proper papers back, the doorbell often rang at eleven o'clock at night, and eyes seeking help looked at me pleadingly. No problem. I sometimes even wrote the lists out myself if the poor people had no idea how to go about it.

One day, a lawyer's representative greeted me rapturously with, "Hey, Lottchen," as if we had been to bed together, except I couldn't remember him at all. Full of mistrust, I entered the apartment in which I was to make my assessment: antique objects as far as the eye could reach. The alleged owners stood, awkwardly looking on, next to a painting from the Biedermeier era. I felt suspicious to the roots of my hair. A few other shapes to whom I had not even been introduced were lounging about in the room. I could see no connection between the allegedly married couple who seemed all wrong somehow—they were so unlikely a pair—and the lovelessly heaped up antiques on the table. They were arranged as if they had been brought to the house expressly for that purpose. Under the Argus-eyes of the people standing about, I assessed everything with Prussian correctness and said good-bye as if nothing were strange.

Soon after that, the eager representative again appeared at my door with a selection of historic table clocks, some of them Oriental, some East Asian, some from the European middle ages. Their unbelievably high value was obvious, and I suspected that they could only be part of an expropriated or stolen private collection, if not museum property. They allegedly belonged to a private individual.

The representative wanted me to give him precise evaluations.

"I can't give you that," I explained, "you must have them assessed at a special museum."

Surely I could give approximate prices, he persisted.

"Whether I say five, fifty, five hundred or five thousand marks, one is as big a lie as the other because I simply don't know."

He left in a bad mood and never came back.

Beginning with 1988, the districts changed their assessors from day to day. Even when the assessments had been made and the owners were sitting on their packed suitcases and trunks, they had to unpack everything and have it reevaluated. If they happened to hit on an assessor who liked to torment people, they would not be able to meet the deadline set by state security for their exit visa and were thus forced to leave everything behind. How often my co-worker Beate and I were forced to go to hastily abandoned apartments whose owners had been unable to complete the formalities. It reminded me of the times I entered the apartments of Jews who were forced to leave everything lying around. True, people in the DDR were on their way to freedom and not being deported to concentration camps, but the stale air, the furniture, half-packed, half in its place—it all awakened sickening memories.

Chapter 25

"PAY ATTENTION ALL OF YOU, we'll be filming a movie here with the title *Coming Out*. Who feels like being in it?" One evening in 1988, at the Burgfrieden, a gay bar in Prenzlauer Berg, Director Heiner Carow was looking for people to take small parts in the first, and last, emancipated gay film to be made in the DDR. I was going to play the role of a barmaid in that particular bar.

My congratulations to Heiner Carow for this important film. Endless difficulties delayed the project for years. The Secretary of the ZK could barely make himself say yes through pursed lips. "You have to put it up for review," he declared in his sharp, professorial way, and even Margot Honecker, as Minister of Education, had to add her absolutely unnecessary opinion. Heiner Carow had to spend more time as diplomat and negotiator than as film director. Nevertheless, he completed even that job valiantly.

We filmed almost exclusively at night since most of the actors had other theatrical engagements. Filming often lasted until four in the morning. But it was worth it. Not only because the showings were sold out for weeks and the film garnered the Silver Bear at the Berlin festival in 1990, but because Carow had, with great sensitivity, depicted gay life in the DDR in a moving way. The plot of the film—one of the two main characters is brought to the hospital in an ambulance because he tried to take his own life—distressed me because it recalled the many suicides among us in the gay community.

Dressed to the hilt, I slipped into the East Berlin Filmtheater International on the day of the premiere. The foyer was full of people. But this evening another "coming out" held the stage of world events. While I was putting on a dress in Mahlsdorf, the Berlin chief of the SED, Günter Schabowski, gave the unforgettable press conference that made thousands of East Berliners run to the wall when it was over.

Right after the premiere ended, there were whispers and rumors. The wall is open? "Hey, guys, no April fool's jokes, today is the ninth of November," I answered.

I could not believe it, although I had had high hopes for weeks. This state, under its age-old, stubborn leadership was not ready for concessions, and would thus rapidly accelerate its own collapse. Alert contemporaries had long noticed the sickeningly sweet stench of something rotting in the weird spectral spectacle of the fortieth birthday celebration of the DDR.

"If you lock your children behind this door," I had said a few years earlier, in a stranger's empty apartment during an official evaluation, when a custom official, a straight-forward man from Mecklenburg, proud of the two stars on his shoulder, asked me why everybody wanted to go to the West, "if you lock your children behind this door and tell them, 'You may not leave!' What will happen? Your children will gather around the door and try to look through the keyhole, and when they are old enough they will try to pick the lock to get the door open. After they have seen what's outside, the secret will be gone and they will come back." But behind such sayings, the senile and dull-witted functionaries, always fleeing from the people by hiding behind the curtains of their Volvos and living in their Wandlitz ghetto as if on another star, suspected only riot, obstinacy, and counter-revolution.

Coming Out was a huge success, and after the premiere it moved in all splendor and suitable acclaim to the Burgfrieden.

Suddenly—voices, honking, confusion. The entire Schönhauser Allée in gridlock with East German Trabi automobiles on the way to the Ku'damm.

The impossible had happened. Shouting with joy as if released from bondage, the people in the bar fell around each other's necks. Finally free! I was happy for the young, but I am not inclined to euphoric outbursts of feeling. So I sat at my table in quiet happiness.

I had just picked up some potato salad with my fork, when a television team burst through the door and a reporter held a microphone, as big as a tennis ball, in front of my nose, "What do you think about it?"

I was so flustered with fright, that I in turn asked, "You mean all the cars outside going to the West?"

"Yes, naturally."

"Well, they'll all cross over, look at the Ku'damm, and be back by tomorrow morning."

Chapter 26

I NEVER NEEDED TO HAVE A "COMING OUT." I never worried about who I was. Everything seemed natural. I knew, "I can't be any other way," even when the school bullies called me a "red-blond goat" and pulled the hair clips out of my hair.

I also had no need to dress up fancy. I still wear size 44, with small shoulders and a stately behind which can fill some things out very well. I prefer gray-green, dark and sky blue dresses, as well as black. I never wear make-up and don't dye my hair. Let others adorn themselves with attention-getting jewelry. I am what I am. Most of the time, I wear an apron and a kerchief and am satisfied to be a housemaid.

For my sixty-third birthday, Beate and Silvia, the lesbian pair who take care of the museum with me, gave me two peasant skirts that are my great pride. The last piece of clothing I bought for myself was a dark blue ladies' coat for the winter. In the mid-seventies, I went to a ladies' tailor in Köpenick with the fabric.

"Well, these days everybody only wears loose coats," the small old man explained after I described the old-fashioned style I had in mind and spread out the roll of fabric on the table. "You're still pretty slim for someone your age, but you don't have much bosom left," he said in a nasal voice, fussing over me with the measuring tape. I had to laugh to myself. "Should I pad the bosom out a little?" he asked sympathetically.

"Sure, go right ahead." I gave directions during the fitting, "Here it could be a little tighter."

"Then it will really flare out here."

"Yes, yes, I like it flared."

"Good, then I'll make the darts a little narrower."

The coat still occupies a place of honor in my wardrobe. I get it out of my walnut cupboard only for special occasions.

It has always been dangerous to go around the streets dressed as a transvestite. I am glad that during the Third Reich I was still very young and so was spared.

Even in the days of the DDR, I didn't fit into any slot, and today I am still an odd figure to some. I always went my own way, a walk on a narrow ridge often with an abyss to the right and left. The endless army of those willing to adapt to a given situation tries to hide behind whatever the circumstances are, and believes them to be inevitable and fated. Better to mistrust such dubious submission since it means falling into the hands of the powerful who like to give their frequently offensive machinations and triumphs the aura of inevitability.

True, it is not granted to everyone to live independently, but with persistence and courage much can be attained, except among the narrow-minded.

Without my doing anything to make it happen, I have become a kind of idol to gays and lesbians. That is the ray of sunshine in which I warm myself in the fall. It is good to know that the way I have lived has given other people some strength.

A year ago, I was at the Brandenburg Gate during a demonstration opposing violence against gays. I was delighted that I had been asked to speak, and before I had even said anything, excited applause began. I was pleasantly surprised at the warm reception given to me; I'm not presumptuous enough to think that I am important.

I can't walk around with my nose in the air. We are all only human beings, whether dairy maid or queen. Let's admit we are all equal. Each little bit of flesh and bones is not so special.

My dream: nobody asks about religion, color of skin, philosophy of life, sexual orientation, political party, wealth or social position. Jews and Christians, heteros and homos, blacks and whites are seated at a beautiful round table outdoors, telling each other ancient stories. And nobody is arrogant or repeats what was blabbed at the taverns. Nobody is suspicious of the other.

In the early seventies, five guys—they are brave in packs—called out to me from the other side of the street as I was looking in the windows of a ladies' dress shop, "Hey, you gay pig, a creature like you would have been burned in Hitler's day. They should drown you in the Ostsee."

I took no notice. Idiots exist everywhere. And compared to the dangers I was exposed to before 1945, most of the discrimination today seems harmless. But one must be on guard against the early signs.

Many good things also happened to me. In July, I allowed myself to take a vacation, the second in my life. Some gay friends had invited me to come to Hamburg. I walked along the Reeperbahn, sipped my pea soup with the whores at a cafeteria at the Grossen Freiheit for two marks, sauntered further, and when I stopped at a shop, I noticed that an older couple was suddenly staring at me with open interest. I could see that they had grown old together peacefully.

The wife cautiously plucked at my sleeve, greeted me and said, "We've seen you on TV. Do you mind if my husband takes a picture of you and me here on the Reeperbahn?"

"No, I don't mind."

Click. "We wish you many good things in your life."

Things like that are so touching.

What do I still wish for? Not much. I am a happy person on the whole. Some time ago, I thought that I had perhaps been born too late, that I would rather have lived at the turn of the century. But no, Prussian militarism would have forced me to go to Capri, where many had to go to avoid conscription. And despite all the disagreements and intolerance, it is surely easier to live as an outsider today than it was in the era of Kaiser Wilhelm.

Chapter 27

I KNOW THAT NO CHILD BLOOMS IN VAIN. Still, I have never found the great love of my life. I say it without regret because "absolute" love, "until death do you part" is nonsense. In earlier times, people lived with one another, worked together and had their pleasures. There may also have been some passion. Love is, after all, a part of life. But I have never thought of life as being only a *part* of love. Everybody knows, without being fully aware of it, what would happen to a "great love" if you had to live in straitened circumstances in a prefab house for three years.

I had my passions. I was close to three men, some of them at the same time, for over twenty years. They helped me, advised me, encouraged me in bad times. We had exciting sex, but an all-consuming passion it was not. I'm not willing to let someone enter my every pore, and it would probably not be very healthy. Anyway, I'm already taken. If I were to get a new Vertikow cabinet today, ten willing men could do cartwheels on my steps and I would send them home. "My dears, come back tomorrow. I don't have any time today," I would call out to them, "because I have to polish my new treasure and find a good place to put it."

During my first love affair, I thought, *Oh, this is so beautiful! This will last my entire life.* When I got older, that changed. It is wrong to become fixated, to chase after the dream man or dream woman. People change and learn; the horizon widens.

With the men in my life, I experienced much more than sex. Was it love? Regardless, there was tenderness, affection, and trust.

I have always found it enriching to be open, to share sex among three people. With no jealousy. Once, when Tutti confessed to me, "I would explode with jealousy," I answered, "If you try to be too controlling, it doesn't work."

If Jochen often acted as my adviser, Werner and Gerhard—the other two men with whom my relationships lasted more than twenty years— took on the roles of comforters.

Werner had strong feminine tendencies and often ran around in drag. When I entered his apartment, which he had furnished with a lot of knick-knacks and a bird twittering in a cage, it was like being in the room of an elderly spinster.

Yet he was the active partner in our relationship. He liked my feminine passivity. "You know, you're like a girl, but you have the figure of a beautiful boy," he would compliment me. I gave in to his wishes. *If he wants me to wear short pants, let him have them,* I thought. That naturally led to ludicrous occasions when one part of the outfit did not go with the other. Once, when we were meandering around Potsdam, some young people called after us, "Look, a woman in short leather pants!" I was wearing high heels with short black pants.

I would have loved to fulfill the dream of sharing bed and board with some of my friends. But that could not be realized because my life was so different from theirs. "Lottchen, to move in with you in these surroundings—no electric lights, no bath, an iron from the year 1890—that's not for me," Werner told me and went back to his new apartment house in East Berlin. In 1984, he had a heart attack and died.

My friendship with Gerhard, whom, like Jochen, I had met at a teahouse, lasted until his death in 1977. He had his moods and whims, was a fanatic about punctuality, but also a warm-hearted human being. He was a strong man, with a robust laugh. I would lower my eyes shyly, like a woman, and feel safe and secure.

Chapter 28

WE CITIZENS OF THE DDR pinned many expectations on the collapse of the wall: that we would become free people in a free country, in a real and true democracy; that the unpleasantness and misery which we had been forced to bear would be confined to the past.

I gave myself over to the hope of finally becoming the rightful owner of the house I had saved. And after some bureaucratic delay, it really seemed about to happen. One day before the currency revaluation, I was driven in a car to a notary public with a lady from the finance section of the Public Property Office. On the way there, she casually mentioned that only the house was to be sold, not the grounds. They had not yet been measured. But I was to buy the planting done by the Bureau of Gardens, as well as the electrical connections to the house, not only already paid for by me, but also wired by me. The notary advised us that unmeasured property could also be purchased. But no! The ground on which the house stood was not for sale. The lady from the magistrate's office remained adamant.

I thought the house-sale chapter closed at least, but I had not taken the overburdened Estate Registry Office, which in those days was drowning in applications, into consideration.

Three days after the attack by the Neo-Nazis—although statements were taken from two apparent perpetrators that night, the inquiry to this day has gotten nowhere—a new assault on the case of the house was made, this time by representatives from the Berlin Senate.

On the Monday after the skinhead attack, a colleague of the museum director called on us. *Terrific!* Beate, Silvia and I decided—finally a ray of light. They also want to help us, just like the representatives from the Senate for Homosexual Lifestyles and the many friends who encouraged us and gave us their support the day after the attack.

The museum expert from the Senate's Department of Culture did not come alone. In addition to a colleague and Professor Bothe from the Berlin Museum, who was favorably inclined towards me, he had also brought along someone without whose help he obviously did not think he could manage. This man had apparently survived the change in government without any trouble. Although his boss was no longer the magistrate, but the Senate, he still occupied the same position: Manfred Maurer.

After the museum expert and his company took seats in the big hall, he came right to the point. "Let's talk facts now. The house does not belong to you." According to his legal advisers, the purchase had not been entered in the registry by the day fixed, that of the union of the two Germanys. It was not his fault, after all, he hadn't signed the Reunion Contract, and if I don't like it, I could hire a lawyer and sue the Berlin government for damages.

I ran from the hall, leaving the guests sitting there. I didn't give a damn about courtesy and etiquette at that moment. I was reminded of the year 1974. *You're being dispossessed and there's nothing you can do about it,* I thought. My nerves were raw anyway. The Neo-Nazi attack still stuck in my craw, and more importantly, my mother, the human being who meant the most to me, had died a few weeks before.

Although I knew that the nature of things meant that all blossoms must wilt sometime, I felt an emptiness after her death and was distraught for days. That she had peacefully gone to her rest was my only small comfort.

Up to the very end, she had done everything herself, worked in the garden and taken care of the household. I visited her the evening before her death. She was in good spirits and cheerful as always. On Easter Sunday 1991, she went to her daughter's room saying she didn't feel well. She sat down on the bed and then lay down.

"Should I call a doctor?" my sister asked, concerned.

"No, no, it will pass right away," my mother answered, unassuming as always. In ten minutes, she was gone.

We never had any disagreements. We instinctively understood each other. Often when I would say something, she would laugh, "That's exactly what I was going to say!" When I turned forty, my mother said, sitting down next to me at the table, "As much as I like to have you with me, you are now really at an age to get married."

My answer, "I am my own wife," left her smiling.

Completely overwrought, I wanted to go to the cellar where Beate and an acquaintance were sitting. I only made it half-way down the steps before my legs almost gave way, and I had to hold on to the banister. "Do you know who's here?" I asked trembling. "Maurer."

I went back to the grand hall with Beate. There, as the museum expert repeated the facts of the case, I suddenly felt ill. Circles were dancing in front of my eyes, and I was close to fainting. I had to lie down in the next room. Professor Bothe timorously suggested that they all leave, but did not succeed.

When I came to, I heard whispering and the humming of voices like a swarm of gnats next door. *Is that guy still sitting there?* I thought angrily. I stood up at once, searched through my cupboard and got out the 1974 document. I burst into the room and told him off. "Comrade Maurer," I said, "you, who wanted to destroy this museum, aren't you ashamed to sit at this table?" My fury was directed only at him. "Shall I read you what you said about me and this museum on February 1, 1974?" Without reaction, he only looked down, small and bent over. A man of character, but certainly not a good one. A man with such a thick hide that he obviously didn't need any backbone. A time-server.

He could have explained to the museum expert from the very beginning that it might not be a good idea for him to come along to Mahlsdorf. His days as head of the Märkische Museum were numbered anyway. If he had at least brought out a word of apology at that moment, I would have been the first to accept it. But no, silent as an air-dried fish, he sat in his chair.

I saw red. I blew a fuse. I tore open the folding doors and shouted, "Get out, you pigs!" Disconcerted, they all looked at each other and stood up. I was determined to hit Maurer around the ears with the protocol of 1974 still in my hand. Beate and Silvia, who knew exactly when my pot boiled over, grabbed my arms from both sides so that I could not move. And the more I wanted to brandish the file, the tighter their grip became.

Only Professor Bothe stayed behind. He had not known about my fight with Maurer in the past, nor about his plotting. Bothe was touched, sympathized with me, and behaved like a human being.

"Nothing is holding me back any more. There are tolerant countries that would be delighted to have me bring my museum. Holland or Denmark, for example," I publicly announced a few days later, and that had its effect.

That's what the crazy Berfeldes are like: with force you get nowhere with me, with friendliness almost everywhere. The Senate indicated it was ready to make a deal.

We live on my six hundred fifty-eight mark pension and on whatever the visitors to the museum donate. I have lived my entire life modestly, almost on the edge of poverty. Mainly plum jam, white cheese, potato salad, and, now and then, some fish. Nothing else. I have my friends, and I get my reward when year-round, six thousand visitors walk through the rooms and say, "Isn't that beautiful!" Because that's what it is: pleasurable, sad, and beautiful. And a little funny, a little touching, and a little educational.

For twenty-five years, I have lived in this house alone. Now we are a team of three, a homo-community. Beate has lived here for nine years, her wife Silvia—they were married by a Danish clergyman on August 20, 1992—for five years. The three of us will continue to preserve and take care of this museum. The Senate has in the meantime assured us that the museum will remain in our hands.

I have slowly reached an age in which one likes to rest a little. But we still have a few plans that we hope to realize with the support of the Senate. The roof and cellar have to be fixed up, the façade restored. We want to make an open-air museum in the garden and reconstruct the stairway on the park side in a historically correct way.

Chapter 29

"It does me honor and gives me great pleasure to present you with the Service Cross on the Ribbon of Merit for service to the German Bundesrepublik in the name of the President of the Republic. Please contact my office to set a date for the proceedings." This letter from the Senator of Culture, with the laconic last sentence, fluttered unexpectedly into my house at the end of June 1992. *So, in my old days I shall become distinguished,* I thought, and had to smile because it seemed a bit comical. But it is a nice gesture that would not have been possible in DDR days.

"After all, you don't work," they threw in my face during the proceedings before the magistrate on February 1, 1974.

"What, all the work I do is not work?"

"No!"

"Well, then you come to Mahlsdorf for a week and do the cleaning, not to mention all the other work, then you'll appreciate how much needs to be done." The official DDR believed me to be "anti-social."

When the Senator arrived, I was in the reception room in my apron, trying to give the chairs a final swipe with my dust rag.

The expression of Ulrich Roloff-Momins, the Berlin Senator of Culture, who had buried his hands in his pants pockets and was regarding the chandeliers with a down-turned mouth, brightened perceptibly when I showed him my collection. My impression was that the private tour gave him pleasure. In the ladies' salon, he took me amicably aside, "It would have been much nicer if the document had been made out in the name of 'Charlotte von Mahlsdorf.'" They had entered my civil name on the letter in Bonn.

The Senator found appreciative words of gratitude, without flattery, just to my taste. A simple address, without exaggeration, but from the heart.

The conferring of this honor was only the overture to the crowning of my difficult labor. Four days later, I received the letter I longed for from the Schöneberg County Court: the entry into the registry was now official. Since August 17, 1992, I have been the owner of the house on Hultschiner Damm 333 in Berlin-Mahlsdorf.

I am an optimist. I believe in the triumph of goodness even if it is sometimes slow in coming. That idea has often kept me alive. The Berlin Senate, I am sure, will be on our museum's side. Eventually the city will inherit everything, since we can't take anything with us into the cold grave—the last garment has no pockets. The city of Berlin has, in this house and this museum, a golden egg. It only needs a bit of cleaning up. As long as I'm alive, naturally, I'll take care of it.

"Children, don't go through the world shut tight like a suitcase. You have to absorb everything: people, nature, houses," my good teacher would always cheer us on. I have taken that advice to heart and have absorbed everything into my soul in these hundred and twenty years—for after all, I have been alive since the Gründerzeit.